RAY LAMPE'S Big Green Egg COOKBOOK

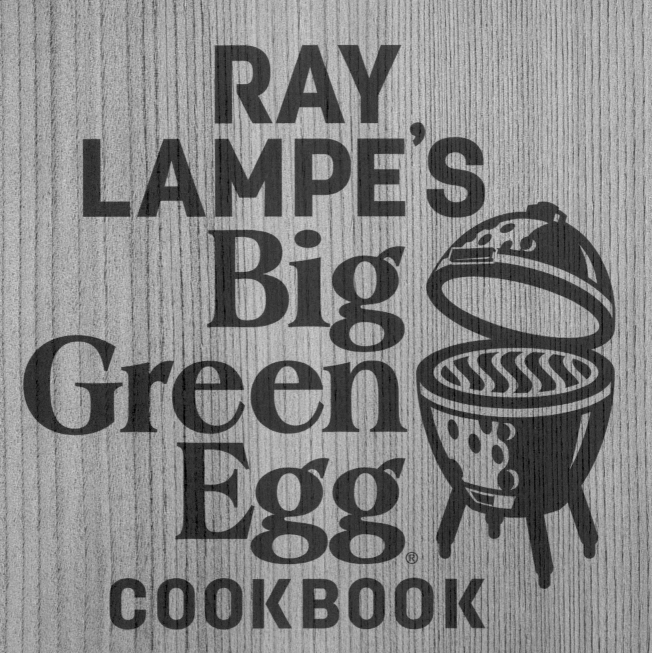

RAY LAMPE'S

Big Green Egg

COOKBOOK

GRILL, SMOKE, BAKE & ROAST

RAY "DR. BBQ" LAMPE

PHOTOGRAPHY BY ANGIE MOSIER

Andrews McMeel

PUBLISHING®

This book is dedicated to Ed Fisher, founder of the Big Green Egg and the original EGGhead. Without his vision and entrepreneurial spirit, we wouldn't be having all of this fun.

Contents

Acknowledgments

Foreword by Jodi Burson

CHAPTER 1: **The EGG and I**   1

CHAPTER 2: **The EGG Carton**   5

CHAPTER 3: **Grilling**

Chicken Wings with Pink Sauce 18

EGGzpacho 19

Flat-Iron Steak Salad 20

Grilled Watermelon Salad 22

Grilled Peach and Serrano Salsa................. 24

Crispy Lobster Quesadilla 25

Fiery Swordfish Tacos............................... 26

Boom Boom Shrimp Wraps 27

Bacon and Egg Cheeseburgers.................... 29

Sliders with Homemade Italian Sausage......30

Triple Pork Burgers..31

Pork Tenderloin with
    Maple Whiskey Glaze 32

Better Than Any Steak House Rib Eye...........33

Filet Mignon with Blue Cheese Butter...........35

Grilled Tri-Tip with Chunky Steak Sauce 36

Lamb Chops with Mint-Cilantro Pesto 37

Porterhouse Pork Chops with
    Savory Grilled Pears....................................38

Rib Eye Pork Chops with Charred
    Ranchero Sauce 40

Grilled Veal Chops with Parmesan Grits 42

Fiery Jerk Chicken Legs 43

Cabo-rita Chicken Tacos................................44

Spatchcocked and Grilled Cornish Hens 46

Grilled Sweet Corn with Fun Butter..............48

Sandi's Fave Grilled Asparagus....................49

CHAPTER 4: **Smoking**

Florida-Style Smoked Fish Spread 52

Smoke-Kissed Deviled Eggs..........................53

Smoked Jalapeño Hummus...........................54

Ham and Swiss Cheese Poppers 55

Chorizo and Shrimpo Fundido......................57

Smokin' Almonds...58

Smoked White Beans
   with Turkey and Kale................................59

Barbecue Beef Sammiches 60

Chunky Chili Con Carne 62

Dr. BBQ's Smoked Meatball Gumbo 65

Brined and Smoked Turkey Thighs...............67

Baby Back Ribs
   with Cookie Butter Barbecue Sauce 68

Memphis Dry-Rubbed
   St. Louis–Style Ribs.................................70

Tender and Tasty Pork Steaks.......................72

Texas-Style Beef Brisket 73

Red Chile Brisket...74

Beef Tips in Double Onion Gravy 75

EGG Smoked Salmon......................................77

Barbecued Pork Shoulder
   with Carolina Sauce 78

CHAPTER 5: **Baking**

Blueberry French Toast Casserole.................82

Ginny and Kim's Thin-Crust Pizza Dough.....85

Ginny and Kim's Deep-Dish Pizza Dough 86

Ginny and Kim's Pizza Sauce........................87

Deep-Dish Tourist Pizza 88

Thin-Crust Real Chicago Pizza......................90

Ginny and Kim's Dessert Pizza 92

Fully Loaded Calzone....................................94

Homemade Garlic Knots 97

Pepper Jelly Meat Loaf Cupcakes 98

Southern Chicken Bog...................................99

Mac and Cheeseburger Casserole...............100

Scalloped Potatoes with Ham 101

Summertime Zucchini Pie............................102

Ham and Cheese Toasty...............................104

Baked Lobster Tails 105

Swiss Cheesy Double-Baked Potatoes........106

Stuffmuffins 107

White Chocolate Chip–Cherry Cookies.......109

Green Velvet Cake..110

Tennessee Honey-Caramel Pecan Pie.........111

Wrapped S'mores...112

Caramel Baked Apples.................................113

CHAPTER 6: Roasting

EGG Roasted Garlic Soup............................116

Porchetta-Style Pork Roast.........................118

Gyro Meatballs with Tzatziki......................119

Herbed-Up Prime Rib..................................120

Roasted Pork Picnic.....................................122

Roasted Ham Glazed
   with Cabo Barbecue Sauce......................123

Sunday Roast Beef.......................................124

Pot Roast with Potatoes and Carrots...........125

Leg of Lamb à la Julia 127

Hot-Roasted Crispy Chicken Thighs............128

Happy Thanksgiving Turkey........................129

EGG Roasted Duck.......................................130

Little Red Potatoes 132

Roasted Head of Cauliflower.......................133

Roasted Butternut Squash 135

Roasted Brussels Sprouts with Bacon.........136

Christmas Chestnuts....................................138

Classic Pork Roast.......................................139

Metric Conversions and Equivalents................141

Index 142

ACKNOWLEDGMENTS

Writing a Big Green Egg cookbook has been a bucket-list item for me, and I couldn't be happier that we finally got it done. It really does take a team. A special thanks to Dr. van Gelder for fixing up my heart so I'd be here to write it. Thanks to Ed Fisher for creating this amazing product and the company around it. I'm proud to be a part of the family. Many thanks to Jodi Burson and Ardy Arani at Big Green Egg and to Jean Lucas and Kirsty Melville at Andrews McMeel for making it happen. Thanks to Scott Mendel for always figuring out a way for me to do the book that I want to do. Thanks to Angie Mosier for the great photography and to Julie Barnes for the equally great design. It would be just a Word document without you both. And finally, thanks to Sandi and my family for letting me work at home and for putting up with me while I do. I wouldn't want it any other way.

RAY LAMPE HAS ALWAYS BEEN A PART OF MY LIFE AT BIG GREEN EGG.

From my first day on the job, he has been there. This enigma, this larger than life personality has been there with me along the way, teaching me about cooking on the EGG, introducing me to incredible characters—and all of the key players—in the grilling world. But most important, he has always been a supporter of my journey from novice EGGhead to his partner in marketing this incredible product that we both love so much.

While the Big Green Egg has many fans—many of them quite famous for their culinary skills—Ray is uniquely qualified to write this cookbook because he has been intimately involved with the company and the evolution of the EGG for many years. He is always first up to test new prototypes and EGGcessories, and his input has been invaluable. So it's no surprise to me that, as I read this book, I felt Ray's passion for cooking on the Big Green Egg, and I knew that I was reading the ultimate guide to

helping you create all of the incredible recipes that the EGG can produce. From grilling and roasting to smoking and baking, Ray explains all of these techniques in an easy-to-understand manner; and just as he did for me, he'll have you cooking like an EGGspert in no time!

Ray and I have been on some incredible adventures together. I've been his sidekick as he's cooked his way around the world, and now he is sharing all of those secrets in this cookbook. I've watched with pride as Ray has evolved from that quirky guy in the flame-decorated pants to an esteemed member of the Barbecue Hall of Fame.

For thirteen years, Ray has been my companion, my mentor, and my confidante. I am honored that he calls me his friend, and I'm even more honored to introduce you to his fantastic collection of recipes in this book. Enjoy!

— **Jodi Burson**
Director of Brand Enhancement

Chapter 1

The EGG and I

"*The Egg and I*, first published in 1945, is a humorous memoir by American author Betty MacDonald about her adventures and travels as a young wife on a chicken farm . . ." That's the *Wikipedia* description of the original book by this title. Although I'm sure it's a good story, I'm also sure it doesn't include much in the way of outdoor cooking, quality meat selection, spice blending, culinary travel, cooking awards, or tequila. My version of *The EGG and I* covers all of these very well. But we both seem to share the love of the EGG. My favorite is the Big Green version. But I must admit that it wasn't always that way. When the world of Internet forums was in its early days, there was a very busy one called The BBQ Forum and another similar one called The Big Green Egg Forum. The BBQ Forum was mostly made up of macho guys from the barbecue competition world, and I was one of them. The Big Green Egg Forum was all EGGheads, and they talked in a friendly, folksy way about how great the EGG was and about all the different things they cooked on it. I found this kind of funny because I didn't think this EGG could possibly be that good.

THE CHICKEN WING THAT CHANGED MY LIFE

I had closed the Lampe family trucking business in 2000 after a great sixty-five-year run and was looking for something new to do with my life. I'd been involved in the barbecue competition world since the very early days, and I had a room full of trophies, so I decided that barbecue would be my next career. I moved from Chicago to Florida and tried what seemed like every possible business that involved the word *barbecue*, unfortunately all with mediocre success. But my life as a barbecue competitor continued strong. I was a force in the early days of the Florida BBQ Association, and my reputation as a barbecue badass was intact. I just needed to figure out how to turn that into a job.

While discussing the world of barbecue one day with my friend Nick Nicholas, we cooked up the idea of me being a barbecue spokesman for a grill company. Grill companies were really beginning to grow, and we convinced ourselves that they were going to need high-profile cooks on their teams. So Nick introduced me to a successful gas grill company from Canada that bought into our vision. They hired me to cook at a couple of barbecue trade shows, and it worked. All of a sudden a guy with a notable culinary reputation and a chef's jacket was cooking next to the typical golf shirt–wearing grill salesman. This was a good idea, and people lined up to see what I was cooking. But the gas grill just wasn't for me. I wanted the food to be better, and I knew that it would be if I was cooking with charcoal.

At one of the trade shows, I happened to be set up next to the Big Green Egg guys. No chef over there, just guys in green golf shirts passing out chicken wings. They knew who I was based on my Internet activity making fun of them, but they were the ever-confident EGGheads, and they wanted me to try their food. Brian Tompkins from Big Green Egg Canada brought me a chicken wing, and I ate it. As we hung out next to one another that day, we all became friends and exchanged business cards.

A few months later, in spring of 2003, I was heading through Atlanta and thought that maybe I should give these folks a call. I rang up one of the guys I'd met, we chatted, and then he offered to give me an EGG to try out. Of course I said yes, and a few days later, I swung by, picked it up, and soon started using it to cook my competition chicken. And I did well! I reported back, and the Big Green Egg folks agreed to mention me to their distributors to see if they had any interest in using me for promotional events. The gas grill company had faded away, and this was my new opportunity.

THE BASEBALL BAT TROPHY

One day I got a call from the Big Green Egg folks in Indiana asking if I could attend a barbecue contest in Kentucky with them and help promote the EGG there. I upped the game by asking if they could bring a few extra EGGs that I could use to cook the whole contest on Big Green Eggs. This had never been done before. Jeff Raymond was the rep for that area and still is. He rustled up the EGGs for me to use, and the local dealer brought another eight or ten new ones to sell. I cooked the contest against all the big hitters of the day who were quite puzzled as to why I'd left my big metal smoker at home to cook on these quirky green things—until I beat them all and won the first-ever Pro Barbecue Grand Championship cooked on only Big Green Eggs. The trophy was an engraved Louisville Slugger bat that is in my office right now.

That was the day that I realized there really was something special about these EGGs. Over at the dealer's booth, only one of the EGGs had been sold before the awards ceremony, and it wasn't looking like a great day. But once I was handed the grand champion baseball bat trophy, the line formed, and both the new EGGs and the ones I'd been cooking on were all sold. We made a lot of believers that day.

THEY SAID YES!

That win in Kentucky qualified me for the big postseason World Barbecue Championship in Tennessee, so I had another idea. If Big Green Egg would put me on a monthly allowance to be the EGG Chef, I would use all EGGs again at the World Championship and beyond. They said yes, and the relationship was born. When this book hits the stores, that relationship with Big Green Egg will be thirteen years old, and we all still like each other. I'm proud of the growth that I have been part of both for the EGG and for me personally. It's been a great partnership and an amazing ride, with a lot of fun and a lot of good people.

Lou West was my early Big Green Egg contact, and we traveled a lot of roads together teaching dealers how to cook on and sell the Big Green Egg. I have cooked a lot of food in the Big Green Egg booth at the big grill-industry trade shows, too—different things, fun things that nobody else was cooking on the grill. This was working, and I believe we changed the industry by doing that. It wasn't long before every grill manufacturer was bringing a ringer chef along to cook. But I had one big advantage: I was cooking on the Big Green Egg, and those other chefs weren't.

A GUY AND A GIRL WALK INTO A BAR

As the company grew, my role evolved into that of a traditional spokesman. At the same time, the world of barbecue was becoming a big deal across the board. My cookbook career was blossoming too, and as I traveled to promote my books, I brought the Big Green Egg along. Because I was a senior member of the competition barbecue community, I was asked to do all of the television shows that were recognizing us as real culinarians, and I always included the EGG.

One day while supporting an event in Chicago, I found myself in a bar with Jodi Burson, marketing director at Big Green Egg. We were discussing how things were changing and decided that we needed to step up our marketing game. We had this phenomenal product, and it was our job to share it with the world, but neither of us wanted to do it the old-fashioned way. There was the EGGhead culture that had happened organically, and we needed to embrace it and celebrate it. The groundwork had been laid long ago by Ed Fisher when he founded the company, and it was now our job to carry the torch. Of course, I fit in well with the nontraditional plan. My background wasn't as a salesman or a chef, and I didn't have a southern barbecue family history. I was a truck driver from Chicago with a silly beard and a shirt with flames on it.

Since that day, we have done a lot of unique and fun marketing things while always remembering who we are. We are EGGheads first. We get the joke. We wear green clothes. I bake green cakes. It may seem kooky, but it works. We're selling EGGs and having fun doing it.

THE NEXT LEVEL

The grill and smoker industry continues to grow and Big Green Egg has become a force. It really does cook better than the rest, and that's the main reason for all of the success. The company has moved into a nice building and added employees, but the personality remains the same. I'm proud to have played a part in the success, and I hope to continue on the journey for a long time. Spreading the gospel of the EGG is a fun and rewarding life. It has taken me to all corners of the United States, and nowadays it takes me all over the world. But the best part is that even after thirteen years, I still look forward to lighting the EGG every single time. Whether I'm at home or firing up the EGG for a couple of hundred EGGheads, I can't wait to get cooking!

Chapter 2

The EGG Carton

In this chapter, I will discuss the ingredients and tools that I like to use when I'm cooking on the Big Green Egg. Although at its core the EGG is an uncomplicated charcoal grill, it's also much more. The simple and ancient design has stood up for literally centuries to cook direct, indirect, on the grid, or on the ceramic. The most important EGGcessory is the convEGGtor. This simple tool converts the EGG from a direct grill to an indirect oven/barbecue pit. It's also critical in cooking pizza, as you'll learn a little later in this chapter. You'll need an ash tool to remove the ash and stir the charcoal before reloading. Beyond that I'm not really a gadget guy. You won't see me using the fad-of-the-month tools or even many of the old reliables. Thermometers are important, and I like to use a cast iron *plancha* (griddle) or Dutch oven occasionally, but most of my food is cooked in a single layer directly on the cooking grid.

The EGG comes in multiple sizes. At the time of this writing, seven models, ranging from the Mini to the XXLarge, are available. But the Large EGG, with its 18¼-inch grid, is the original, and it's my favorite. It's also the most popular, so for the recipes in this book, I have used the Large EGG exclusively. It would be confusing to try to include the nuances of making each recipe in each different-size EGG. All of the other sizes work equally well, and you shouldn't have any problem using the recipes with a little common EGG sense.

Today's EGG is similar in design to the originals that Mr. Fisher imported many years ago. There is a base, a top, a hinge/handle, a fire box, a fire ring, a charcoal grate, and a cooking grid. That's pretty much all there is to an EGG. Add a bottom sliding vent door and a top vent cap and it's ready to go. The variety of things that you can do with this simple design is truly amazing. So let's get started.

The first thing that you need to do is load the EGG with charcoal. Lump charcoal is all you should ever use. Briquettes are full of chemicals and will create too much ash and interfere with the great airflow that makes the EGG cook so well. The good news is that lump charcoal lights easily and makes the food taste great. If you're starting with a clean, empty EGG, all you do is pour the charcoal straight from the bag, filling up to the top of the

fire box. This is the standard fill for most cooking. If you've cooked on your EGG previously and have leftover charcoal, the first thing you need to do is to stir the old coals with your ash tool so the ash drops to the bottom. Then you can add new charcoal to bring the level to the top of the fire box. After that, I like to stir the old and the new to mix them together.

For most of my cooking, I have found that lump charcoal gives the food enough of a smoky flavor. If you like more smoke, you can add some wood chips or chunks to the charcoal before lighting. I don't find a need to soak the chips or chunks. If I want just a light smoke, I use chips. First I load half of my charcoal, then I spread an even layer of wood chips on top, and then I add the rest of the charcoal on top of that. A couple of handfuls of wood chips will do it. If I want a stronger smoke for a longer cook like brisket or pork butt, I use chunks. Two or three chunks that total about the size of my fist are enough. I never use more wood than this, and I never add additional wood later in the cook.

If you load the EGG as I've described, you should never need to add charcoal during cooking. If you find yourself running out, you simply need to add more charcoal at start-up. If you like your food smokier, add more wood at the beginning but beware: Most folks don't really like their food heavily smoked. If anyone tells you the food is too smoky, it probably is. Cooks gets desensitized to it after breathing it for the long cooking time, so they don't taste it as strongly as others do. Start with less wood; you can always add more next time. Undersmoked food is still very good. Oversmoked food is not enjoyed by anyone.

WHAT KIND OF WOOD?

These are the woods I like and use. You may find others locally, and if you prefer them, you should use them.

APPLE: A light, sweet smoke flavor. Use alone or paired with hickory or oak when cooking chicken, turkey, fish, pork, or beef.

CHERRY: A light, sweet smoke flavor. Use alone or paired with hickory or oak when cooking chicken, turkey, fish, pork, or beef.

HICKORY: A strong smoke flavor but classic barbecue taste. Use sparingly with chicken or turkey. Use alone or paired with a milder wood like apple or cherry with pork or beef.

OAK: A medium-strong smoke flavor but classic barbecue taste. Use sparingly on chicken and turkey. Use alone or paired with a milder wood like apple or cherry with pork or beef.

PECAN: A middle-of-the-road taste and strength. Pecan seems to go well with everything when used in moderation and is my favorite.

ASH MANAGEMENT

Ash management and lighting the EGG go together because you never want to remove the ash when the EGG is hot. When you are done cooking, close the air vent in the lid and the air vent in the base to shut down the airflow fully. Leave the EGG alone, and the fire will go out, and the EGG will cool down in a couple of hours. The next time you want to cook on your EGG, just open both air vents completely. Remove the cooking grid and set it aside. Stir the cooled coals to allow the ash to drop to the bottom of the EGG. Insert the Big Green Egg ash tool into the bottom vent door, and scrape out the ash into a disposable pan or onto a piece of cardboard or aluminum foil. It's simple when everything has cooled down but would be very dangerous with a hot EGG and a live fire.

When all of the ash is scraped out, you're ready to light the fire. You don't have to remove the ash from the EGG before every cook, but you should do it after every three or four. One caveat to this routine is that every now and then you should use up or remove all of the charcoal from your EGG for a full clean out. If you don't, the reused charcoal will eventually become a lot of tiny pieces that will impede airflow. I'd suggest doing this about every fifteen times you use the EGG. Your mileage may vary depending on how you cook, but if your EGG isn't getting hot, it's probably because ash buildup is restricting proper airflow.

TOP VENT   **BOTTOM VENT**

LIGHTING THE EGG

Big Green Egg sells natural charcoal starters, small, square, flat pieces of paraffin and sawdust. You tuck one into the lump charcoal and light the corner. These work really well, and I recommend them. But I think they work best when broken in half. I find that three halves evenly spaced and tucked into the charcoal do a good job of lighting a large EGG. There are many ways to light an EGG, and if you have a different technique that's working for you, go for it! Just don't ever use liquid lighter fluid. It will make your EGG stinky for a long time. After I light the charcoal starters, I add the convEGGtor if I'm using it and then I replace the cooking grid. Next, I leave everything alone and open for 10 minutes. Then I close the lid of the EGG but leave the bottom and top vents wide open for another 5 minutes. Finally, I open the EGG and brush the grid with a wire grill brush. Once the grid is cleaned up, I close the vents halfway and start working toward my desired cooking temperature.

HOW DO I GET THE DESIRED COOKING TEMPERATURE?

That's the million-dollar question. The answer seems so simple to those of us who have been doing it for a long time, but it can seem a bit intimidating to the folks who are just getting started. Here are a few tips before I describe the procedure.

1. Try to sneak up on the desired cooking temperature gradually.

2. Remember that you're also heating up the ceramic mass, so it will take a little time.

3. Don't get crazy over 5 to 10 degrees either way.

4. Give the temperature a little time to settle rather than constantly making minor adjustments.

5. Adding air by opening up the vents raises the temperature and closing off the air cools the EGG down.

6. You'll figure it out pretty quickly, but if all else fails, buy a Big Green Egg DigiQ.

Light the EGG as previously directed or using your preferred method. Read rule number 1. It's much easier to bring the temperature up a little than to bring it down. The rise may seem slow on the way up because you are warming the ceramic mass of the EGG along with the air inside. Have patience and read rule number 2. Now read rule number 5 two times. If the EGG gets too hot, do not open the lid to let the heat out. That's just not how it works. In fact, that's the opposite of how it works. Adding air fuels the fire and heats things up. Keeping the lid closed and closing down the vents a bit calms the fire and cools the EGG down. But it takes time. Read rule number 4 again.

To cook at 350°F, the basic position is half open for the bottom vent and about 1 inch of a gap for of air through the top vent. That's not the gospel. Every fire and every EGG are a little different, but that's a starting point. Adjust from there, remembering that if you open both vents a little, the fire will get hotter, and if you close them a little, it will get cooler. I tend to think of the top vent as a good tool for small adjustments and the bottom vent as a tool for bigger adjustments. Now read rules number 1, 3, 4, and 5 again. And if all else fails, read rule number 6. The Big Green Egg DigiQ is a great tool and I use it often. In case you don't know what it is, it's an automatic temperature-control device that uses a probe, a little fan, and a mini computer to maintain the temperature precisely where you want it. I use it for overnight long cooking so I don't have to check my temperature in the middle of the night, and I use it on busy days like Thanksgiving when I'm in the kitchen prepping other dishes and I don't want to be concerned with the turkey. It's a great tool, but for most of us and for most cooking, it's not required.

So my suggestion is to get cooking. As long as you use good technique and a temperature gauge for deciding when the food is done, you'll be eating well. The recipes will help you with that, and with a little practice, you'll be a pro in no time.

LID OPEN OR CLOSED?

The Big Green Egg burns and cooks best with the lid closed. The bottom and top air vents work together to create an even, hot environment that helps keep food moist and juicy. Unless I specifically say to cook with the lid open, you should close the lid during all cooking. On rare occasions, I will cook with the lid open, but this is an extreme method. For example, if I want to sear a thin steak or chop without cooking it from the top down, this works well. However, you must never, ever walk away from your EGG when the lid is open. The EGG can get very hot very quickly when the lid is left open, and when you close it, the risk of a flashback is high.

WHAT'S A FLASHBACK?

The Big Green Egg is a great environment in which to build a hot fire. It also seals well to control the fire via limited oxygen flow. But when you quickly close off the oxygen to a hot fire and then quickly reintroduce it, you get what is called a flashback or backdraft. It's easily managed by "burping" the EGG as you open it. Just open the lid a couple of inches and hold it there for a few seconds. This allows the incoming air to enter slowly and helps prevent a flashback from happening. After that, just open the lid slowly and go about your cooking. You should burp the EGG whenever you are cooking above 350°F; it will quickly become a habit, and you won't even realize that you're doing it.

COMMON EGG COOKING SETUPS

I use only a few simple setups to cook on the EGG. I know that some of you have elaborate rigs and like to cook a little differently, and I think that's great. I like it simple, and I think the EGG works best that way. We are all right as long as we're cooking on an EGG and using good technique to know when the food is done. Here are my recommendations.

Direct

This is the most common setup and is used for all direct grilling. Fill the fire box to the top with lump charcoal. Light it and replace the cooking grid. Follow my instructions for reaching your desired temperature on page 8 or do it your way. It may seem like a lot of charcoal, but you'll be able to control the temperature by how much air you let in. When you're done cooking, close the air vent in the lid and the air vent in the base, and the EGG will go out, saving the leftover charcoal for next time.

Indirect with Drip Pan

Adding the convEGGtor to the EGG for indirect cooking makes it work like a convection oven, with a barrier between the direct heat and the food. Indirect with a drip pan is the primary setup for smoking and roasting. The drip pan will catch any dripping fat and prevent it from burning on the convEGGtor and also from falling onto the charcoal. Some cooks like to add liquid to the drip pan, but I don't think it adds anything but a mess to clean up. For this setup, fill the fire box to the top with lump charcoal, adding smoking wood if you are using it. Light the charcoal the same as always, putting in the convEGGtor as soon as the fire is lit. I usually cover the convEGGtor with aluminum foil to keep it clean, but most EGGheads don't bother with this.

Indirect without Drip Pan

This is exactly the same setup as indirect with a drip pan but is used for things that are cooked in a pan or just won't drip, like cakes, cookies, or pizzas. No harm is done if you want to add a drip pan. It just isn't necessary.

DIRECT　　　　　**INDIRECT**

GOOD TECHNIQUE TO KNOW WHEN THE FOOD IS DONE

I've mentioned the importance of taking the food out of the EGG at the perfect time more than once, so I need to explain. Taking the food off at the perfect time is the most important thing you can do in any cooking. If the EGG temperature is a little hot or a little cool, the food will still be fine. It will just take a little more or a little less time to cook. Because of this, you cannot decide when food is done by timing alone. Every fire is a little different. Every piece of meat is a little different, too. It may be a little thicker or thinner or warmer or colder when it goes in the EGG. All of this will affect the cooking time. The best way to determine when food is done is to use your eyes, your finger, and a thermometer.

Look at the food. Does it look done? Only experience will tell you this, so pay attention and gain that experience. Touch the food. Poke it with your finger. Stick a fork in it. Raw meat is soft and mushy. Overcooked meat is firm. Perfect meat just begins to offer resistance. Once again, experience will make you an expert, so get started by poking everything you cook. Last but not least, you need to get a good instant-read thermometer, and you need to use it. Check the meat in a few places, and when it's done, take it off and eat it. If you practice all of these techniques you will be serving perfectly cooked food. Here are some suggested doneness temperatures.

Chicken breast 160°F

Chicken legs, thighs, and wings 180°F

Turkey breast 160°F

Turkey legs, thighs, and wings 180°F

Pork chops, tenderloins, and other lean cuts 150°F

Pork shoulder for tender pulled pork 200°F

Beef steaks and roasts rare 120°F

Beef steaks and roasts medium-rare 125°F

Beef brisket 200°F

Ground beef 155°F

Lamb chops and racks medium-rare 135°F

MY FAVORITE THINGS

In general I try to use common tools and ingredients that you might already have or you can buy pretty easily. You'll never see me using the gadget of the month or hard-to-find ingredients, but I do buy quality tools that last. I really believe that the EGG can do most of what I want by itself. There are a few exceptions that really do make the difference. Here are my favorite things.

TOOLS

I always have a box of nitrile gloves near my EGG. First thing I do when I go out to my EGG is put on a pair. I can grab the dirty grid, handle some charcoal, or pick up a messy convEGGtor with no worries. When I'm done, I take the gloves off, toss them, and my hands are clean.

My tongs are relatively short and spring-loaded. Big barbecue tongs can sometimes be awkward, making it hard to move things around. When cooking over a really hot fire, I will make an exception and use long tongs or a pig tail food flipper.

I use the Big Green Egg digital high-speed model food thermometer. Speed is key, and this one is really fast.

My knives are an assortment of high-quality Shun knives. They are beautiful and they perform well. I prefer these over the heavier German-style knives, but whichever style and brand you choose, you should buy good knives and take care of them.

I use big white polyethlene cutting boards.

I use big silicone mitts for grabbing hot grids and even the convEGGtor.

I use the Big Green Egg perforated grids in different sizes for handling small or soft things like seafood and vegetables.

I use a cast-iron Dutch oven for soups, stews, and chili.

I use the Big Green Egg 14-inch pizza stone and the 14-inch deep-dish pizza stone.

I use a round metal pizza pan as a baking sheet.

I go through a lot of disposable aluminum foil pans, using them to cook and hold foods and as drip pans. You can mess them up and throw them away. I buy them by the stack at a warehouse club.

I use a Vitamix blender.

I use a Cuisinart 8-cup food processor.

I use a KitchenAid stand mixer to make pizza and cookie dough.

I use the DigiQ by Big Green Egg for temperature control.

I use a small electronic kitchen scale.

I use Big Green Egg lump charcoal. It's a quality blend of hickory and oak wood, and I think it's very good stuff.

To get the fire started, I use Big Green Egg natural square charcoal starters.

INGREDIENTS

I use Morton brand coarse kosher salt unless otherwise specified and restaurant-grind black pepper.

I'm a snob about chili powder. I like the San Antonio red blend from Pendery's in Fort Worth. They have plenty of others for different tastes, and they are all better than the stuff at the supermarket. While I'm ordering, I also buy granulated garlic, granulated onion, ground cumin, cayenne pepper, paprika, and dried herbs from them. Everything that Pendery's stocks is high quality and worth ordering. The seasonings are shipped in sealed bags, so be sure to order some shakers from them, too (www.penderys.com). I use King Arthur's all-purpose and bread flours.

I buy most of my meats at the warehouse club or supermarket. If you have a source for great local meats and the price works for you, go for it. Every region is different, so roll with what you have available. My beef typically comes from the supermarket or warehouse club, and it's choice grade. I do like USDA prime steaks for special occasions. If you can't find great steaks locally, check out my friends at the Kansas City Steak Company (www.kansascitysteaks.com).

My pork typically comes from the supermarket or warehouse club. My chicken will come from whoever sells it without injecting. Look for the 5 percent enhanced kind of warning on the label and stay away from that if you can.

My seafood comes from a local fishmonger that sells a lot of it. Fresh is the key.

Produce is also all about fresh. If you have a great local farmers' market, use it. If not, shop at the store with the best-looking fresh produce. Buy what looks good that day and adjust your menu to fit it.

GET COOKING!

So we've discussed the EGG, its setups, charcoal, wood, tools, and ingredients. But none of that is worth a darn if you don't season the food properly. Although many of the recipes in this book include a dry rub that works well with that dish, don't be afraid to mix and match if something sounds good. It's the same with sauces and glazes. Nothing makes me happier than knowing that you tweak my recipes to fit your own tastes, be it small tweaks or big overhauls. I may be the Big Green Egg "spokeschef," but I'm surely not the only cook that makes great food on the EGG.

Cook things the way you and your family like them. You can also use store-bought rubs and sauces, and there are a lot of great small-batch ones are available. Big Green Egg makes some great sauces, and even some of the big brands turn out some pretty tasty products. Try what's available, and if you and your guests find something you like, I suggest that you keep using it. And if you have that secret family recipe, well I know you're going to keep using that.

The one message I want to share before you start cooking any of my recipes is to make them your own. These are my recipes the way I like them. I want you to make them the way you like them, and that way we'll both be very happy.

Chapter 3

Grilling

Grilling is the art of cooking directly over a wood fire. It has to be the origin of all cooking. No caveman made a skillet before he put a piece of meat directly over a fire. As I wrote in my first book, an accidental sun-dried tomato may have preceded grilling, but until archaeologists discover that's the case, I will contend that grilling is the origin of all cooking. At first glance the Big Green Egg is simply a grill: a nice environment for a lump charcoal fire in the bottom with a grid to suspend the food over it. The concept was probably invented about the same time as the wheel. But along the way, man perfected it with the excellent airflow of an EGG fire box and the mass of ceramic that helps with even heat and fuel conservation. The caveman only dreamed of such a great grill.

In this book, I will show you all of the advanced cooking techniques possible with the EGG, but you must never underestimate its prowess as a great and simple grill. Many EGGheads won't go to a steak house anymore after perfecting their home steak technique. They brag about saving money on steaks to spend on better wine. Steaks, glorious steaks, and chops and burgers and sausages are what the grill

was made for. And when I was a kid, those were the only foods that ever crossed the grill. My dad would roll the chuck wagon grill out of the garage for special occasions and cook the steaks. This was pretty much the norm in all households. Mom would take care of everything else, and Dad would hope for the best. My father wasn't much of a cook, so I really can't imagine how he knew when the steaks were done, but he sometimes got lucky. He knew nothing of the Big Green Egg and wouldn't have even imagined grilling things like fruits, vegetables, or desserts.

But things have changed, and they've changed a lot. Great chefs and great grilling equipment have taught us that we can add grill flavor to many things right in the backyard. Quality charcoal, natural charcoal starters, instant-read thermometers, and grills that allow you to control the temperature make it possible to grill just about anything that you cook in the kitchen. And it all tastes better. In this chapter, you will find some fun new ideas next to the steaks, chops, and burgers. Pay attention to the techniques and don't feel obligated to cook the recipes exactly as they are written. We all like things done a little differently, so go ahead and make them your own.

Everybody loves grilled chicken wings, and there are many great ways to make them. In the EGG, you can slow grill them directly like I have in this recipe or cook them indirect. Both ways work well. I always use whole wings that look like they were recently attached to a chicken. I like big, meaty wings, and I like to sauce them after cooking. This pink sauce is a tasty combo of a white barbecue sauce like my friends up in Alabama make mixed with a little sweet red barbecue sauce. Add a bit more horseradish if you dare. I like to serve these with celery sticks.

Chicken Wings with Pink Sauce MAKES 4 TO 6 SERVINGS

12 whole chicken wings

RUB

2 teaspoons kosher salt

1 teaspoon paprika

1 teaspoon black pepper

½ teaspoon granulated onion

½ teaspoon granulated garlic

PINK SAUCE

1 cup mayonnaise

Juice of ½ lemon

¼ cup ranch dressing

¼ cup sweet barbecue sauce

2 tablespoons prepared horseradish

2 tablespoons honey

½ teaspoon kosher salt

½ teaspoon black pepper

Prepare the EGG to cook direct at 350°F. Cut the tips off of the chicken wings and discard them. With a sharp knife, slash the skin on the inside of the joint. To make the rub, in a small bowl, combine all of the ingredients and mix well. Season the wings on all sides with the rub, using all of it.

Place the wings on the EGG cooking grid, and cook, flipping the wings occasionally, for about 30 minutes, or until they are golden brown on both sides and have reached an internal temperature of 200°F.

Meanwhile, make the sauce. Combine all of the ingredients in a medium bowl and mix well.

When the wings are done, transfer them to a deep dish or a large bowl. Pour half of the sauce over the wings, toss well to coat, and transfer to a clean platter. Serve with the remaining sauce for dipping.

Chilled vegetable soup on a hot day can only get better when the vegetables get a little kiss of flavor from a visit to the EGG. Grill them just until they have a little char; there's no need to cook them until they are tender. For a change of pace, I like to do two half batches of the gazpacho in the food processor, one puréed and one a little chunky, and then mix them together for an interesting texture. Serve the soup really cold, or let it warm a bit before serving. Never serve it hot, however. To dress things up try garnishing with a little sour cream and some chopped cucumber.

MAKES ABOUT 8 SERVINGS **EGGzpacho**

Prepare the EGG to cook direct at 500°F. Place the onion, cucumber, tomatoes, celery, and chile in a shallow pan. Drizzle with the oil and season with ½ teaspoon of the salt and ¼ teaspoon of the pepper. Toss to coat evenly.

Place the onion and celery on the EGG cooking grid and grill, turning them as needed, for 2 to 3 minutes, until lightly charred on all sides. Return them to the pan. If the onion comes apart, grill the layers until browned. At the same time, place the cucumber, tomatoes, and chile, skin side down, on the grid and grill for 2 to 3 minutes, until charred brown on the skin side. Return them to the pan.

Coarsely chop the celery and cucumber. Place half of the vegetables in a food processor fitted with the metal blade. Add 1 cup of the V8 juice, 1 table-spoon of the vinegar, ½ teaspoon of the salt, ¼ teaspoon of the granulated garlic, and ¼ teaspoon of the black pepper and process for 10 seconds. Check the texture and process for another 10 seconds if you want a smoother texture. Transfer to a large bowl. Add the remaining vegetables, 1 cup of the V8 juice, and the remaining 1 tablespoon vinegar, ½ teaspoon salt, ¼ teaspoon granulated garlic, and ¼ teaspoon pepper to the processor and process for 10 seconds. Check the texture and process for another 10 seconds if you want a smoother texture. Add to the bowl holding the first batch and then add the remaining 1 cup V8 juice. Using a large spoon, stir until fully blended. Check for salt and pepper and add some if needed. Cover and refrigerate for at least 4 hours before serving. Serve cold or cool.

½ medium red onion, halved lengthwise

1 medium cucumber, halved lengthwise

6 large Roma tomatoes, halved lengthwise and seeded

2 stalks celery

1 jalapeño chile, halved lengthwise

2 tablespoons olive oil

1½ teaspoons salt, divided

¾ teaspoon black pepper, divided

3 cups V8 juice, divided

2 tablespoons red wine vinegar, divided

½ teaspoon granulated garlic, divided

When you think of a Dr. BBQ Big Green Egg salad, you don't expect some wimpy microgreen dish, and I'm not going to disappoint you. I always put some meat in my salad, and for this one, I was thinking about steak house—friendly ingredients like spinach, tomatoes, and smoked Gouda. Flat-iron steak is delicious and a pretty good bargain in the steak world. Just don't overcook it, and be sure to slice it thinly against the grain. You could even skip the greens and still have a good salad.

Flat-Iron Steak Salad MAKES 4 TO 6 SERVINGS

1 (12-ounce) flat-iron steak

RUB

½ teaspoon kosher salt

¼ teaspoon black pepper

¼ teaspoon granulated garlic

¼ teaspoon granulated onion

¼ teaspoon dried basil leaves

BROWN SUGAR VINAIGRETTE

½ cup olive oil

3 tablespoons balsamic vinegar

1 clove garlic, crushed

½ teaspoon kosher salt

¼ teaspoon black pepper

¼ teaspoon dried basil leaves

1 tablespoon firmly packed
  brown sugar

5 ounces mixed salad greens
  (such as spring mix, arugula,
  red leaf, and romaine)

5 ounces baby spinach leaves

5 green onions, white and firm
  green parts, thinly sliced
  on the diagonal

1 medium carrot, peeled
  and julienned

1 medium beefsteak tomato,
  cut into wedges

1 cup shredded smoked Gouda
  cheese

Prepare the EGG to cook direct at 500°F. Take the steak out of the refrigerator 30 minutes before you plan to cook it. To make the rub, combine all of the ingredients in a small bowl and mix well. Season the steak on both sides with the rub, using it all. Let the steak rest for 5 minutes so the rub will adhere.

To make the vinaigrette, combine all of the ingredients in a blender and blend on medium speed for 30 seconds, or until emulsified. Leave the dressing in the blender.

Place the steak on the EGG cooking grid and cook with the lid open for 3 to 4 minutes, until golden brown on the bottom. Flip the steak and continue cooking for 3 to 4 minutes with the lid open, until golden brown on the second side. Flip the steak one more time, close the lid and cook for another 1 to 2 minutes, until it reaches an internal temperature of 125°F in the center. Transfer to a plate and let rest for 5 minutes.

Place the greens, spinach, green onions, and carrot in a large salad bowl and toss well. Blend the dressing on high speed for 15 seconds. Pour the dressing over the greens and toss to coat well. Sprinkle the cheese evenly over the salad, then arrange the tomato wedges around the edge of the salad. Slice the steak thinly against the grain and place the slices on top of the salad. When ready to serve, gently toss the whole salad to incorporate everything evenly.

When you've been cooking on the EGG for as long as I have, you get around to grilling just about everything. Watermelon may seem like a weird candidate for the EGG, but the sweet taste actually pairs nicely with a little wood flavor. Watermelon is mostly water, so it won't brown very well, but it will pick up a smoky quality. As with so many ingredients, this works best when watermelon is in season and sweet, firm ones are available. If some nice heirloom tomatoes are in the market, be sure to use them instead of the little yellow ones I call for here.

Grilled Watermelon Salad MAKES 6 SERVINGS

2 slabs seedless watermelon, about 1 by 4 by 6 inches

DRESSING

3 tablespoons extra-virgin olive oil

2 tablespoons balsamic vinegar

½ teaspoon kosher salt

¼ teaspoon black pepper

6 cups spring mix

¼ medium red onion, thinly sliced

2 cups halved mini yellow tomatoes

10 fresh mint leaves, cut in chiffonade

½ cup crumbled Gorgonzola cheese

¼ cup sunflower seeds

Prepare the EGG to cook direct at 550°F. Pat the watermelon dry with paper towels. Place the watermelon on the EGG cooking grid and cook for 2 minutes, or until lightly browned on the first side. Flip the watermelon and cook for another 2 minutes, or until lightly browned on the second side. Transfer the watermelon to a plate and let cool completely.

Cut the watermelon into bite-size cubes (about 1-inch cubes). You should have about 2 cups.

To make the dressing, combine all of the ingredients in a medium bowl and whisk until well blended.

Place the spring mix in a big salad bowl. Drizzle two-thirds of the dressing over the greens and toss well. Add the onion, tomatoes, mint, cheese, and sunflower seeds and toss well. If more dressing is desired, add it now and toss again. Scatter the watermelon over the top, toss lightly, and serve.

Salsa is easy to make if you can get someone else to do all the chopping for you. But even if you can't, it's well worth the effort. To make great salsa, you need a distinctive hot chile and a sweet fruit to counter it. Peach and serrano are my favorite pairing. Grilling the ingredients makes them all a little sweeter and mellows out the whole bowl like nothing you can buy in the store. For the best flavor, make the salsa a couple of hours ahead and let it rest, if you can resist eating it.

Grilled Peach and Serrano Salsa MAKES 6 SERVINGS

6 large Roma tomatoes, halved lengthwise and seeded

½ medium white onion, halved lengthwise

2 peaches, pitted and quartered

1 serrano chile, halved lengthwise and seeded

1 poblano chile, halved lengthwise and seeded

½ teaspoon salt, plus more for seasoning vegetables and peaches

Juice of 1 lime

⅓ cup chopped fresh cilantro

½ teaspoon black pepper

Prepare the EGG to cook direct at 500°F. Lay the tomatoes, onion, peaches, and serrano and poblano chiles on a large sheet pan. Season them with salt on all sides. You will grill all of these ingredients together, but each one needs a little different plan. Place them on the cooking grid. Grill the tomatoes skin side down for 2 to 3 minutes, until most of the skin is charred dark brown. Flip the tomatoes and cook for 1 minute. The second side won't brown because it is too moist. Transfer to a platter. Grill the onion and peaches, flipping them occasionally, for 4 to 5 minutes, until golden brown on all sides. Return the onion and peaches to the pan. Grill the serrano and poblano chiles skin side down for 2 to 3 minutes, until the skin is charred dark brown. Remove to the pan. Set aside to cool for 10 minutes.

Chop the tomatoes into small dice. Transfer to a strainer placed over a bowl and let drain while you cut the other ingredients. Remove as much skin as possible from the poblano chile and cut the chile into small dice. Place it in a medium bowl. Remove as much skin as possible from the serrano chile, mince it, and add it to the bowl. Cut the onion and peaches into small dice and add them to the bowl. Add the drained tomatoes to the bowl along with the ½ teaspoon salt, the lime juice, cilantro, and pepper. Toss well. Let sit for 5 minutes and toss again. Check for salt and add some if needed.

Imagine if the lobster roll was invented south of the border and was actually cooked in a toasty tortilla and had a cheesy, peppery lobster and green onion filling. I did that one day and this was the end result. I like this served hot or at room temperature, so it's great tailgating food. You can substitute shrimp for the lobster if you prefer and just about any herb for the tarragon. To top off this quesadilla in a decadent way, serve it with freshly made guacamole and with sour cream.

Crispy Lobster
MAKES 4 TO 6 SERVINGS **Quesadilla**

Prepare the EGG to cook direct at 350°F. Using sharp kitchen shears, cut the lobster shell lengthwise from end to end and carefully lift out the meat. Cut the meat in half lengthwise. Place the lobster meat on the EGG cooking grid and cook, turning once, for 4 to 5 minutes on each side, until the meat is opaque. Set aside to cool.

Place the pizza stone in the EGG to preheat for 15 minutes. In a medium bowl, combine the green onions, tomato, chiles, tarragon, and lemon zest. Season lightly with salt and pepper and toss to mix. Lay the tortillas flat on a work surface. Using about half of the cheese, top half of each tortilla with an equal amount of the cheese. Top the cheese with half of the green onion mixture, dividing it evenly among the tortillas. Slice the lobster meat crosswise into ¼-inch-thick slices. Lay the slices on top of the green onion mixture, dividing them evenly among the tortillas. Finally, top the lobster with the remaining cheese, again dividing it evenly. Fold the empty half of each tortilla over the loaded half.

Carefully lay the quesadillas on the preheated pizza stone and cook for 6 to 7 minutes, until golden brown and crispy on the bottom. Using a large spatula, carefully flip the quesadillas. Cook for another 6 to 7 minutes, until the bottom is golden brown and crispy.

Transfer to a platter and let rest for 3 minutes. Cut each quesadilla into 4 wedges to serve.

1 (8-ounce) lobster tail, thawed if frozen

4 large green onions, white and firm green parts, thinly sliced

1 large Roma tomato, seeded and diced

2 serrano chiles, seeded and minced

1 tablespoon finely chopped fresh tarragon

Finely grated zest of ½ lemon

Kosher salt and black pepper

4 (10-inch) flour tortillas

8 ounces queso panela or Monterey Jack cheese, shredded

Using fish in tacos is a natural in coastal places, so we do it a lot here in Florida. The reason, of course, is because we have plenty of beautiful fresh fish. This recipe calls for swordfish, but as always, you should use what looks good and fresh that day. Mahimahi would be perfect and so would tuna, though I suggest serving the tuna rare. The same is true for the salsa: Use what looks good that day. I like mango, but fresh peaches or pineapple would work well, too.

Fiery Swordfish Tacos MAKES 4 SERVINGS

SALSA

3 medium Roma tomatoes, seeded and cut into small dice

6 green onions, white and firm green parts, thinly sliced

½ mango, cut into small dice

1 jalapeño chile, halved lengthwise and thinly sliced

Juice of ½ lime

½ teaspoon salt

½ cup finely chopped fresh cilantro

RUB

½ teaspoon kosher salt

½ teaspoon paprika

¼ teaspoon black pepper

¼ teaspoon granulated garlic

¼ teaspoon granulated onion

¼ teaspoon cayenne pepper

1 pound swordfish fillets

16 (6-inch) corn tortillas

1 cup finely shredded iceberg lettuce

One hour before you plan to cook, make the salsa. Combine the tomatoes, green onions, mango, and chile in a medium nonreactive bowl. Mix well with a large spoon. Add the lime juice, salt, and cilantro, mix well again, and set aside. If the salsa will be sitting for longer than 1 hour, cover and refrigerate it.

Prepare the EGG to cook direct at 450°F. To make the rub, combine all of the ingredients in a small bowl and mix well. Cut the fish into about ¼-inch-thick pieces so it will have a lot of brown edges when cooked. Season the pieces on all sides with the rub, using it all.

Place the fish on the EGG cooking grid and cook for 4 to 5 minutes, until golden brown on the bottom. Flip the fish and cook for another 4 to 5 minutes, until golden brown on the second side and firm to the touch. Transfer to a plate.

To heat the tortillas, in batches, place them on the cooking grid for just a few seconds on each side. You don't want to brown them. As they are ready, transfer them to a sheet pan, stacking 2 tortillas for each taco.

Using a fork, break up the fish into coarse flakes. Divide the lettuce evenly among the stacked tortillas. Top each taco with a portion of the fish, dividing it evenly. Using a slotted spoon, top the fish with the salsa, dividing it evenly. Serve 2 tacos to each diner.

Nearly every restaurant seems to have a dish like this one on its menu, but most restaurants aren't lucky enough to have an EGG for cooking the shrimp. The light grilled flavor is a welcome addition, and I think my sauce is just a little better than everyone else's, too. Feel free to add a little more Sriracha sauce to spice it up, or use bigger shrimp and serve them over rice.

Boom Boom Shrimp Wraps

MAKES 6 SERVINGS

Soak 6 bamboo skewers in water for 15 minutes, then drain. Prepare the EGG to cook direct at 500°F. Divide the shrimp into 3 equal portions, then thread each portion onto 2 parallel skewers. (Using 2 skewers makes the shrimp easier to turn.) Season the shrimp lightly with salt and pepper.

To make the sauce, combine all of the ingredients in a medium microwave-safe bowl and mix well. Set aside.

Place the shrimp on the EGG and cook for 2 to 3 minutes, until they are opaque on the bottom side. Flip the shrimp and cook for another 2 to 3 minutes, until they are opaque on the second side. Transfer to a plate and let cool for 2 to 3 minutes, until you can handle them.

Heat the sauce in the microwave on high for 30 seconds. Mix well. Remove the shrimp from the skewers, put them in the sauce, and toss to coat well. Place a lettuce leaf on each plate and top each leaf with an equal number of the shrimp. Top the shrimp with a little of the sauce, garnish with the green onions, and serve.

1 pound shrimp (26/30 count), peeled, deveined, and tails removed

Kosher salt and black pepper

SAUCE

½ cup mayonnaise

¼ cup sweet Thai chili sauce

2 teaspoons Sriracha sauce

½ teaspoon black pepper

6 leaves Boston lettuce

2 green onions, white and firm green parts, thinly sliced on the diagonal

This is a great combination for topping a burger, and though it is a little messy to eat, I never seem to get any complaints. If you buy your ground beef at the supermarket, look for "market ground" to get the ground-up trimmings just like the old days. Don't ask where the other stuff is ground or you'll be surprised. I usually cook the bacon and eggs in the house, but they can both be easily cooked outside on the cast-iron *plancha* (griddle) on the EGG.

MAKES 6 SERVINGS Bacon and Egg Cheeseburgers

Prepare the EGG to cook direct at 500°F. Divide the meat into 6 equal portions, form each portion into a ball, and then flatten each ball into a thin patty the size of the buns. Season the patties on both sides with salt and pepper.

To make the sauce, combine the ranch dressing and barbecue sauce in a small bowl and whisk until blended. Set aside.

Place the halves from 1 to 2 rolls, cut side down, on the EGG cooking grid and, working quickly, cook just until browned, about 10 seconds. Set aside on a platter and repeat with the remaining rolls in batches. Place the burgers on the grid and cook for 2 to 3 minutes with the lid open, until well browned. Flip the burgers, close the lid, and cook for another 2 to 3 minutes, until well browned on the second side. Flip the burgers and top each one with a slice of cheese. Close the lid and cook for 1 minute, or until the burgers reach an internal temperature of at least 155°F. Transfer the burgers to a separate platter from the buns. Tent the burgers loosely with aluminum foil to keep warm while cooking the eggs.

Heat a large nonstick skillet over medium-high heat on the stove. Add the bacon fat reserved from cooking the bacon. Break the eggs into the pan and cook for 2 to 3 minutes, until set on the bottom. Flip the eggs and cook another for 2 to 3 minutes, until the whites are fully set.

Meanwhile, spread the bottom of each roll with 2 tablespoons of the sauce. Top with a burger and then with 2 bacon slices. When the eggs are ready, top each burger with an egg and season with salt and pepper. Close with the roll tops and serve.

2 pounds ground beef

Kosher salt and black pepper

SAUCE

¼ cup ranch dressing

¼ cup barbecue sauce

6 onion rolls, split

6 slices American cheese

12 slices bacon, cooked and drippings reserved for cooking eggs

6 large eggs

I grew up in Chicago with plenty of Italian neighborhoods, stores, and restaurants. Italian food is a staple food for most Chicagoans, so when I moved to Florida it was a bit of a culture shock not to have all of those places nearby. My answer is often to make those Italian favorites myself, and one of the easiest and most satisfying is Italian sausage. You can buy ground pork at the supermarket and add a few things to make a very easy and tasty version. I just grill it in patties or meatballs and avoid the hassle of stuffing it in casings.

Sliders with Homemade Italian Sausage MAKES 4 TO 6 SERVINGS

2 pounds ground pork

⅓ cup finely chopped
green bell pepper

1 tablespoon kosher salt

1 tablespoon fennel seeds

1 teaspoon cayenne pepper

½ teaspoon granulated garlic

1 teaspoon dried basil leaves

12 slices fresh mozzarella cheese

12 slices Roma tomato

12 slider buns, split

Prepare the EGG to cook direct at 500°F. Using your hands, break up the pork into small pieces, capturing it in a large bowl. Sprinkle the green pepper, salt, fennel seeds, cayenne, garlic, and basil evenly over the meat. Using your hands, mix the meat until everything is evenly distributed. Divide the mixture into 12 equal portions, form each portion into a ball, and then flatten each ball into a patty slightly larger than the slider buns.

Place the sausage patties on the EGG cooking grid and cook for 3 to 4 minutes, until the bottom is golden brown. Flip the patties and top each with a slice of the cheese. Cook for another 3 to 4 minutes, until the bottom is golden brown and the meat reaches an internal temperature of 160°F.

Remove the patties to a plate and tent loosely with foil. Quickly grill the cut sides of the buns for about 15 seconds until golden brown. Remove to a plate. Top each slider bun bottom with a sausage patty and top each patty with a slice of tomato. Close with the bun top and serve.

Pork burgers are a great but overlooked option in the burger world. Look for "market ground" pork at the supermarket (see Bacon and Egg Cheeseburgers headnote, page 29). If by chance you can't find good ground pork, just buy a hunk of pork shoulder with a lot of fat on it and ask the butcher to grind it for you. For this burger, I've used English muffins. They are a favorite burger bun for me mainly because I don't like a lot of bread. As for the triple-pork idea, well, why not?

MAKES 4 SERVINGS Triple Pork Burgers

Prepare the EGG to cook direct at 500°F. Divide the pork into 4 equal portions and form each portion into a patty just slightly larger than the English muffins. To make the rub, combine all of the ingredients in a small bowl and mix well. Season the pork patties on both sides with the rub, using it all.

Place the Canadian bacon on the EGG cooking grid and grill with the lid open for about 30 seconds on each side to warm, then transfer to a nearby plate. Place the muffins, two at a time, on the grid and grill with the lid open, turning once, for about 30 seconds on each side, or until lightly toasted. Transfer to 4 individual plates. Place the burgers on the grid, close the lid, and cook for 3 to 4 minutes, until golden brown on the bottom. Flip the burgers and top each burger with 1 Canadian bacon slice, 1 cheese slice, and 3 bacon half slices. Close the lid and cook for 4 to 5 minutes, until golden brown on the bottom and the internal temperature reaches 155°F.

Lay a lettuce leaf on each muffin bottom, top it with a burger, and top the burger with a tomato slice. Add a squeeze of barbecue sauce and close with the muffin top.

1 pound ground pork

RUB
½ teaspoon kosher salt
½ teaspoon black pepper
½ teaspoon paprika
¼ teaspoon granulated onion
¼ teaspoon granulated garlic

4 slices Canadian bacon
4 English muffins, split
4 slices Swiss cheese
6 slices bacon, cooked and halved crosswise
4 romaine lettuce leaves
4 tomato slices
Barbecue sauce, for serving

I generally don't use combination ingredients because I'd rather mix my own flavors, but maple whiskey is just too good to ignore. I found that it was best when combined with a little maple syrup to enhance the maple and a little cayenne to spice things up. That's for cooking. It drinks pretty good just the way it's made. Always take care not to overcook pork tenderloin or it will be dry. Use a good instant-read thermometer, cook it to an internal temperature of 145°F, and then let it rest for 3 minutes and it will be perfect.

Pork Tenderloin with Maple Whiskey Glaze MAKES 6 SERVINGS

GLAZE
3 tablespoons salted butter

3 tablespoons all-purpose flour

1½ cups maple whiskey

⅓ cup maple syrup

¼ teaspoon cayenne pepper

RUB
2 teaspoons kosher salt

1 teaspoon black pepper

1 teaspoon granulated onion

1 teaspoon granulated garlic

1 teaspoon paprika

2 whole pork tenderloins, about 2½ pounds total

Prepare the EGG to cook direct at 450°F. To make the glaze, melt the butter in a small pan over medium heat on the stove. Add the flour and stir with a large spoon until blended. Cook for about 1 minute, stirring occasionally until the mixture is hot and bubbling. Add the whiskey, syrup, and cayenne, mix well, and cook, stirring occasionally, for 3 to 4 minutes, until the mixture reaches a simmer. Continue cooking for 2 to 3 minutes, until the mixture is thick enough to coat the back of a spoon. Remove from the heat and set aside.

To make the rub, combine all of the ingredients in a small bowl and mix well. Trim the silver skin and any excess fat from the tenderloins. Season the tenderloins all over with the rub, using it all. Place the pork on the EGG cooking grid and cook for 2 minutes. Flip the pork and brush the top with the glaze. Cook for another 2 minutes. Flip the pork and brush with the glaze. Continue cooking, flipping and glazing every 2 minutes and closing the lid after each turn, until the pork has reached an internal temperature of 145°F. This should take a total of 16 to 18 minutes. If any glaze remains, it must be discarded once the pork comes off the EGG, so try to use all of it while the pork is cooking.

Transfer the pork to a platter, tent loosely with aluminum foil, and let rest for 5 minutes. Slice and serve.

Having a Big Green Egg allows you to make great steaks at home every day. You will lose interest in high-priced steak houses and save a lot of money along the way. An internal temperature of 120°F may seem low, but the carryover is greater when you are cooking very hot than when cooking at low temperatures. I like my steaks at least 1¼ inches thick, which allows me to cook them long enough to get that nice char on the outside without overcooking. If you have light eaters for such a big steak, just have them share or slice the steaks and serve family-style.

Better Than Any Steak House Rib Eye

MAKES 2 TO 4 SERVINGS

One hour before you plan to cook, take the steaks out of the refrigerator. To make the rub, combine all of the ingredients in a small bowl and mix well. Season the steaks evenly on all sides with the rub, using it all, and let the steaks stand at room temperature for the rest of the hour until cooking.

Prepare the EGG to cook direct at 500°F. Place the steaks on the EGG cooking grid, leave the lid open, and cook for about 3 minutes, until the bottoms are well browned. Flip the steaks and close the lid. Cook for another 3 to 4 minutes, until the bottoms are well browned. Continue cooking for 3 to 4 minutes, flipping every minute or so and closing the lid each time, until the steaks reach an internal temperature of 125°F for medium-rare.

Transfer to a platter, tent loosely with aluminum foil, and let rest for 5 minutes. Drizzle with the butter before serving.

2 USDA choice or prime rib eye steaks, about 1¼ inches thick

RUB
1 tablespoon kosher salt
1 teaspoon ground coriander
½ teaspoon black pepper
½ teaspoon granulated garlic
½ teaspoon granulated onion
½ teaspoon chili powder

4 tablespoons salted butter, melted

Filet mignon, or beef tenderloin, is the most tender of all the beef steaks and is very lean. That means that it doesn't have the big beef flavor that the chewier and fattier cuts have, which makes it the perfect candidate for this big-flavor treatment. This recipe is for my friend Marcy at The Kansas City Steak Company. She likes the cinnamon and cayenne additions to this rub that I made to season the company's tasty steaks, and so do I. The blue cheese butter has a really cool look, kind of like a mini mortadella, and is a great addition to these steaks as well.

Filet Mignon with Blue Cheese Butter

MAKES 4 SERVINGS

At least 1 hour or up to 2 days before you plan to cook, make the blue cheese butter. Place the butter in a medium bowl and top it with the pepper, granulated garlic and onion, and chili powder. Using a spoon or silicone spatula, mix until blended. Add the cheese and fold it in, taking care not to break up the crumbles. Lay a 12-inch square of waxed paper on a work surface. Spoon the butter in a log shape onto the waxed paper, positioning it two-thirds of the way down from the top edge. Roll up the log in the waxed paper, then twist the ends to tighten it. Place in the refrigerator to set for at least 1 hour before using.

About 1 hour before you plan to cook, take the steaks out of the refrigerator and leave at room temperature. Prepare the EGG to cook direct at 500°F.

To make the rub, combine all of the ingredients in a small bowl and mix well. Season the steaks on all sides with the rub, using it all. Let the steaks rest for 5 minutes so the rub will adhere. Take the butter out of the refrigerator and slice it into 4 equal pieces. Place the steaks on the EGG cooking grid, leave the lid open, and cook for about 4 minutes, or until golden brown on the bottom. Flip the steaks, cook for 1 minute, and then close the lid. Cook, checking occasionally and flipping if the bottom gets well browned, for 4 to 5 minutes, until golden brown on the bottom and cooked to an internal temperature of 125°F for medium-rare.

Transfer the steaks to a platter and immediately top each steak with a piece of the butter. Let the steaks rest for 3 minutes before serving.

BLUE CHEESE BUTTER
4 tablespoons salted butter, at room temperature
¼ teaspoon black pepper
¼ teaspoon granulated garlic
¼ teaspoon granulated onion
¼ teaspoon chili powder
¼ cup crumbled blue cheese

4 (10-ounce) beef tenderloin fillets

KANSAS CITY STEAK RUB
1 teaspoon kosher salt
½ teaspoon black pepper
½ teaspoon granulated onion
½ teaspoon granulated garlic
½ teaspoon chili powder
¼ teaspoon ground coriander
¼ teaspoon ground cinnamon
¼ teaspoon cayenne pepper

Tri-tip is the beloved barbecue of the folks in Northern California, and when you try it, you'll see why. At 2 to 3 pounds each, it's kind of a steak-roast hybrid that grills beautifully. In California, you'll find tri-tips with or without the fat cap, but the rest of us will typically find them fully trimmed. Either is fine as long as you don't overcook it. There's plenty of internal fat, and the trimmed version will have more of that great grilled crust. Feel free to use your EGG cooking experience on this one and grill it a little hotter if you dare.

Grilled Tri-Tip with Chunky Steak Sauce MAKES ABOUT 4 SERVINGS

RUB

1 teaspoon kosher salt

1 teaspoon black pepper

1 teaspoon granulated garlic

1 teaspoon granulated onion

1 beef tri-tip, about 2½ pounds, fully trimmed

SAUCE

¼ cup olive oil

1 small yellow onion, diced

1 poblano chile, seeded and diced

2 large Roma tomatoes, seeded and diced

2 cloves garlic, crushed

2 tablespoons red wine

1 teaspoon soy sauce

1 teaspoon Worcestershire sauce

2 teaspoons balsamic vinegar

½ teaspoon kosher salt

¼ teaspoon black pepper

Prepare the EGG to cook direct at 400°F. To make the rub, combine all of the ingredients in a small bowl and mix well. Season the tri-tip evenly on all sides with the rub, using it all. Let the tri-tip rest for 10 to 20 minutes so the rub will adhere.

To make the sauce, heat the oil in a medium skillet over medium heat on the stove. Add the onion, chile, tomatoes, and garlic and cook, stirring occasionally, for 4 to 5 minutes, until the onion and chile just begin to soften. Add the wine, soy sauce, Worcestershire sauce, vinegar, salt, and pepper, mix well, and cook for about 1 minute, or until it comes to a simmer. Pour the sauce into a food processor fitted with the metal blade. Pulse 5 or 6 times, or until everything has broken down into a chunky sauce. Transfer to a bowl and set aside.

Place the tri-tip on the EGG cooking grid and cook, flipping the meat occasionally, for about 20 minutes, until well browned on both sides and cooked to an internal temperature of 125°F deep in the center for medium-rare.

Transfer the tri-tip to a platter, tent loosely with aluminum foil, and let rest for 10 minutes. Slice thinly against the grain to serve. Drizzle half of the sauce over the slices and serve the other half on the side.

Many Americans just don't seem to like lamb as much as the rest of the world does, but don't count me on that list. These loin chops are really mild and would be a great place to start eating lamb at home. Grill them just like a steak, and they'll be great. Mint is a natural partner to lamb, so I made a pesto with mint and cilantro to top these with a fresh pop.

Lamb Chops with Mint-Cilantro Pesto

MAKES 4 TO 6 SERVINGS

Prepare the EGG to cook direct at 400°F. Brush the chops lightly all over with olive oil and season liberally with salt and pepper.

To make the pesto, in a blender, combine the mint, cilantro, garlic, almonds, Parmesan, lime juice, salt, and pepper. Start the blender on medium speed and then slowly add the extra-virgin oil. Continue to blend for about 30 seconds, or until puréed. You'll need to stop the blender and scrape down the sides of the pitcher a couple of times. Transfer the pesto to a bowl. Taste for salt and add if needed. Set aside.

Place the chops on the EGG cooking grid, leave the lid open, and cook for 4 to 5 minutes, until golden brown. Flip the chops, close the lid, and cook for 4 to 5 minutes, until golden brown on the second side and cooked to an internal temperature of 130°F for medium-rare.

Transfer the chops to a platter, tent loosely with aluminum foil, and let rest for 5 minutes. Serve 2 or 3 chops, topped with the pesto, to each diner.

12 lamb loin chops, about
 1½ inches thick
Olive oil, for brushing
Kosher salt and black pepper

PESTO
¾ cup fresh mint leaves
¾ cup fresh cilantro leaves
2 cloves garlic, crushed
¼ cup chopped almonds
¼ cup grated Parmesan cheese
Juice of ½ lime
½ teaspoon kosher salt
½ teaspoon black pepper
½ cup extra-virgin olive oil

You can expect recipes like a big grilled porterhouse chop from me, and it certainly works well on the Big Green Egg. But what about these pears? I've always grilled apples but never thought of pears until my friend Lee Anne Whippen cooked some up for me one day. She grilled them and basted them until they were tender and delicious, so I decided to pair them with some pork chops. I'd call it a great match.

Porterhouse Pork Chops with Savory Grilled Pears MAKES 4 SERVINGS

RUB

1 tablespoon paprika

1 tablespoon raw sugar

2 teaspoons kosher salt

1 teaspoon granulated onion

½ teaspoon granulated garlic

½ teaspoon ground cinnamon

¼ teaspoon ground nutmeg

¼ teaspoon cayenne pepper

4 porterhouse pork chops, about 1 inch thick

1 teaspoon olive oil

2 large Bosc pears

6 tablespoons salted butter, melted

Prepare the EGG to cook direct at 400°F. To make the rub, combine all of the ingredients in a small bowl and mix well. Brush the chops with the oil and season them liberally on both sides with the rub, reserving some of the rub for the pears and butter.

Halve the pears lengthwise and, using a melon baller or a small spoon, scoop out the seed area. Season the cut side of each pear lightly with some of the rub. Add the remaining rub to the butter and mix well with a spoon.

Lay the pears, cut side down, on the EGG cooking grid and cook for 5 minutes, or until golden brown. Flip the pears, brush the cut side with the butter mixture, and cook for another 5 minutes, or until the skin side is golden brown. Flip the pears again and move them to the sides of the grid. Brush the skin side of each pear half with the butter mixture.

Place the chops in the center of the grid and cook for 5 minutes, or until the chops are golden brown on the bottom. Flip the chops and the pears. Brush the pears with any remaining butter mixture and cook for about 5 minutes longer, or until the pears are soft and the chops have reached an internal temperature of 145°F for medium-rare or 160°F for medium.

Transfer the chops and pears to a platter and let rest for 3 minutes. Serve 1 chop and 1 pear half to each diner.

My good friend chef Sue Torres gets credit for this idea. I was going to cook on the Food Network's *Chopped Grill Masters* a few years ago, and when talking my ideas through with her, she suggested a grilled ranchero sauce. She told me just to grill up everything and throw it in a blender or food processor. This was great advice because you can hide some less desirable ingredients in there while making a great sauce that is perfect for *Chopped*. I didn't blend it that day, as I wanted it chunky, but it did help me win. Later on, I did the blended version on the show *Food Fighters*. The sauce is great on these chops but would go well on just about any grilled protein.

Rib Eye Pork Chops with Charred Ranchero Sauce MAKES 6 SERVINGS

RUB

2 teaspoons kosher salt

1½ teaspoons black pepper

1½ teaspoons chili powder

6 (1 inch thick) pork rib eye chops

SAUCE

4 Roma tomatoes, halved lengthwise and seeded

1 jalapeño chile, halved lengthwise and seeded

1 serrano chile, halved lengthwise and seeded

1 poblano chile, halved lengthwise and seeded

½ red bell pepper, seeded and halved lengthwise

½ medium red onion, halved lengthwise

4 tablespoons olive oil, divided

1 teaspoon kosher salt, divided

¼ teaspoon black pepper

½ teaspoon chili powder

1 tablespoon fresh cilantro leaves

Juice of ½ lime

Prepare the EGG to cook direct at 400°F. To make the rub, combine all of the ingredients and mix well. Season the pork chops liberally on both sides with the rub, using it all. Set the chops aside.

To make the sauce, place the tomatoes, all of the chiles, the bell pepper, and the onion in a shallow pan. Drizzle with 2 tablespoons of the oil and season with ½ teaspoon of the salt and all of the pepper. Toss to coat evenly. Place the tomatoes, chiles, and bell pepper skin side down and the onion pieces flat side down on the EGG cooking grid. Cook the tomatoes, chiles, and bell pepper until about two-thirds of the skin side is charred. Return them to the pan. Cook the onion, flipping occasionally, until golden brown on all sides. If the onion comes apart, grill the layers until browned. Return the onion to the pan.

Place the pork chops on the EGG cooking grid, leave the lid open, and cook for 2 to 3 minutes, until golden brown. Flip the chops, close the lid, and cook for another 3 to 4 minutes, until golden brown on the bottom. Flip the chops, close the lid, and cook to an internal temperature of 145°F for medium-rare or 160°F for medium, 2 to 3 minutes longer. Transfer the chops to a plate and tent loosely with aluminum foil.

Place the tomatoes, all of the chiles, the bell pepper, and the onion in a blender. Add the remaining 2 tablespoons oil and ½ teaspoon salt along with the chili powder, cilantro, and lime juice. Blend on high speed for 1 minute, or until smooth. Taste for salt and add if needed.

To serve, spoon ¼ cup of the sauce onto a plate and top it with a chop.

Veal chops are a personal favorite when I go to a steak house. They're pricey in the meat case, but they make for a special treat for dinner guests, too. The sweet and mellow flavor pairs well with a bit of Italian flair in the form of garlic, basil, and olive oil. I grill these a little more slowly than a typical red meat chop because of the garlic and oil on the outside and the delicate veal on the inside. I've added a side dish of Parmesan grits here because it pairs so well, but feel free to serve these chops with potatoes if you prefer.

Grilled Veal Chop with Parmesan Grits MAKES 4 SERVINGS

4 veal rib chops, about ¾ inch thick

Kosher salt and black pepper

¼ cup olive oil

4 cloves garlic, crushed

6 large fresh basil leaves, torn

GRITS

2 cups water

2 cups milk, plus more if needed

2 teaspoons kosher salt

1 teaspoon black pepper

1 clove garlic, crushed

1 cup white corn grits

2 tablespoons salted butter

½ cup grated Parmesan cheese

2 large fresh basil leaves, chopped

One hour before you plan to cook, season the chops on all sides with salt and pepper. Pour the oil onto a large plate and mix in the garlic and torn basil. Dredge the chops in the oil mixture and let them rest on the plate, turning them occasionally, for 1 to 2 hours.

Prepare the EGG to cook direct at 400°F. Meanwhile, make the grits. Combine the water, 2 cups milk, salt, pepper, garlic, and grits in a medium saucepan and mix well. Place over medium heat on the stove, bring to a simmer, and cook, stirring often, for 15 to 20 minutes, until the grits are tender, thick, and creamy. Add a little milk along the way if needed to keep a thick, soupy consistency. Add the butter, Parmesan, and chopped basil and stir until the butter and cheese are melted and fully blended. Cover, remove from the heat, and set aside.

Place the chops on the EGG cooking grid and cook for 6 to 8 minutes, until the bottom is golden brown. Flip the chops and cook for another 6 to 8 minutes, until golden brown on the bottom and cooked to an internal temperature of 125°F for medium-rare.

Transfer the chops to a platter and let rest for 5 minutes. Place a spoonful of the grits on each of 4 plates, top each mound of grits with a veal chop, and serve.

This is a unique EGG grilling technique with all the flipping, but that's what the real jerk men do, so play some Bob Marley and embrace it. Scotch bonnet chiles are the staple for jerk in the islands, but we can't always find them in the United States. The good news is that we do always have habaneros, and they're pretty close. If you remove all of the ribs and seeds, you could end up with a mild jerk, however, as every batch of chiles is different. I like to leave the ribs in 1 chile and a scattering of seeds to make sure I get that kick that jerk is known for.

MAKES 4 SERVINGS Fiery Jerk Chicken Legs

A few hours before you plan to cook, make the jerk paste. Put all of the ingredients in a blender and blend on low speed for 15 seconds and then on high speed for about 45 seconds, or until the mixture is smooth. Set aside.

Using a sharp knife, slash each drumstick three times, cutting about ½ inch deep on a 45-degree angle to the bone and spacing the slashes evenly apart. Lay the drumsticks in a glass dish or bowl and pour the jerk mixture over them. Toss the drumsticks around to coat them evenly, making sure to get the mixture into the slashes. Cover and refrigerate for at least 1 hour or up to 4 hours.

Prepare the EGG to cook direct at 350°F. Remove the drumsticks from the jerk marinade, reserving the marinade, and place them on the EGG cooking grid. Cook for 4 minutes. Flip the drumsticks and baste with the reserved marinade. Cook for another 4 minutes. Flip and baste again, using all of the marinade or discarding it at this point. Continue cooking and flipping every 3 to 4 minutes, moving the drumsticks around as needed to ensure even cooking, until they have reached an internal temperature of 180°F when tested deep in the meaty part. The total cooking time should be 35 to 45 minutes.

Transfer the drumsticks to a platter or individual plates and serve.

JERK PASTE

1 cup diced white onion

6 green onions, white and firm green parts, sliced

3 Scotch bonnet or habanero chiles, seeded, ribs removed, and finely chopped

4 cloves garlic, crushed

Juice of 1 lime

2 tablespoons kosher salt

2 tablespoons dark rum

2 tablespoons distilled white vinegar

2 tablespoons peeled and chopped fresh ginger

1 tablespoon soy sauce

1 tablespoon firmly packed light brown sugar

1 tablespoon ground allspice

2 teaspoons dried thyme leaves

1 teaspoon black pepper

½ teaspoon ground cinnamon

½ teaspoon ground nutmeg

8 large chicken drumsticks, about 2½ pounds total

One of my many jobs is as a spokesman for Cabo tequila, and I often do events for Cabo in which I cook on the EGG and use the tequila. Yes, this is any man's dream job. So last year I grilled some Cabo-rita chicken thighs, and the guests liked them when they were sober and really, really liked them later in the day. The recipe is basically grilled chicken with some Cabo margarita poured on it. These make tasty tacos, but you won't want to feed them to the kids.

Cabo-rita Chicken Tacos MAKES 6 SERVINGS

RUB

½ teaspoon kosher salt

½ teaspoon cayenne pepper

¼ teaspoon paprika

¼ teaspoon black pepper

¼ teaspoon granulated onion

¼ teaspoon granulated garlic

1 pound boneless, skinless chicken thighs

SAUCE

¼ cup Cabo Tequila Blanco

2 tablespoons Cointreau liqueur

1 tablespoon agave nectar

Juice of 1 lime

6 (6-inch) flour tortillas

2 large Roma tomatoes, seeded and cut into small dice

¼ cup finely diced red onion

¼ cup coarsely chopped fresh cilantro

1 lime, cut into 6 wedges

Prepare the EGG to cook direct at 450°F. To make the rub, combine all of the ingredients in a small bowl and mix well. Lay the chicken thighs flat and season them on all sides with the rub, using it all.

Place the thighs on the EGG cooking grid and cook for 4 to 5 minutes, until golden brown on the bottom. Flip the thighs and cook for another 4 to 5 minutes, until the second side is golden brown and the thighs have reached an internal temperature of 180°F.

While the thighs are cooking, make the sauce. Combine all of the ingredients in a small bowl and mix well. Set aside.

When the thighs are ready, transfer them to a platter. Let cool until they can be handled, then chop coarsely and place in an EGG-safe pan. Pour the sauce over the chicken and toss to coat evenly. Place the pan on the EGG cooking grid and cook for 4 to 5 minutes, until heated through.

To heat the tortillas, in two batches, place them on the grid for just a few seconds on each side. You don't want to brown them. Lay a tortilla on each of 6 plates. Top each tortilla with an equal portion of the chicken. Top the chicken with equal portions of the tomato, onion, and cilantro. Squeeze a lime wedge over each taco and serve.

Cornish hens are really just mini chickens, but they sure are tasty. I like to brine them so I can cook them without worrying about them drying out, but you can't brine them for too long or they'll get salty and rubbery. The hens are grilled direct, which means you have to keep an eye on them to avoid burning the skin. This extra effort will help you get a crispy, crunchy skin. I don't glaze these hens because I want to preserve that skin, but if you like to glaze yours with barbecue sauce, just brush some on at the end.

Spatchcocked and Grilled Cornish Hens MAKES 2 TO 4 SERVINGS

BRINE

2 cups cold water

½ cup kosher salt

½ cup raw sugar

2 tablespoons lemon pepper

1 tablespoon granulated garlic

1 tablespoon granulated onion

1 teaspoon dried thyme leaves

6 cups ice-cold water

2 Cornish hens

Olive oil, for brushing

Kosher salt and black pepper

At least 8 hours before you plan to cook and preferably the night before, make the brine. Pour the 2 cups cold water into a small saucepan and place over medium-high heat on the stove. Add the salt, sugar, lemon pepper, granulated garlic and onion, and thyme, mix well, and cook, stirring often, for about 8 minutes, or until well blended and just short of a simmer. Place the 6 cups ice water in a large bowl, add the brine mixture, and mix well. Cover and refrigerate for 2 hours.

Meanwhile, using kitchen shears, cut each hen down its back, splitting its backbone. Open each bird and place, split side down, on a cutting board. Flatten each bird by pushing down on it with your hands. Place the hens in a large, heavy-duty resealable plastic bag.

When the brine is ready, whisk it well to blend and then pour it into the bag holding the hens. Seal the bag, pushing out as much air as possible. Place the bag back in the bowl just in case a leak forms. Place the bowl in the refrigerator for 3 hours, flipping the bag 2 or 3 times while it rests.

Remove the hens from the brine, rinse well under cold running water, and then dry them well. Place a rack on a sheet pan and place the hens, split side down, on the rack. Place the sheet pan in the refrigerator and let the hens rest, uncovered, for 3 hours.

Prepare the EGG to cook direct at 400°F. Dry the hens again and brush the skin side with oil. Season the skin side only with salt and pepper. Place the hens, split side down, on the EGG cooking grid and cook for 20 minutes. Flip the hens and cook for 10 minutes longer. Check for browning on the skin and continue checking every 2 to 3 minutes until the skin is well browned. Flip the hens and check their internal temperature. They are done when they have reached an internal temperature of 160°F in the breast and 180°F in the thigh. They may not need any additional cooking at this point, but if they do, cook then split side down until they have reached the desired internal temperature.

Transfer the hens to a platter, tent loosely with aluminum foil, and let rest for 5 minutes before serving.

I'm kind of jumping on the Mexican street-food bandwagon here. I don't like my corn charred, so I cook it in the husk. In Wisconsin, where the best corn ever is grown, cooks soak it in water and leave it whole, so that when it hits the grill, it steams and the kernels become soft and tender. Some peel back the husk first and remove the silk, but I like to leave the husk intact for good steaming. You'll need to clean off all of the silk before eating, of course. As for the fun butter, this recipe is definitely a suggestion, and you should add what you like or what looks good to you that day. After all, it is called *fun* butter.

Grilled Sweet Corn with Fun Butter MAKES 6 SERVINGS

6 ears sweet corn in the husk

FUN BUTTER

½ cup salted butter,
   at room temperature

¼ cup grated Parmesan cheese

½ teaspoon granulated onion

½ teaspoon granulated garlic

½ teaspoon chili powder

¼ teaspoon salt

¼ teaspoon cayenne pepper

Using a sharp knife, cut off the husk at the top of each ear of corn. Discard any loose leaves. Place all of the corn ears in a sink or vessel deep enough to immerse them in water. Cover and top the ears with a plate so they stay submerged. Let them soak for 2 hours.

Meanwhile, make the fun butter. Place the butter in a medium bowl and add the remaining ingredients. Using a spoon, mix the butter with the other ingredients until all of the ingredients are well mixed. Lay a 12-inch square of waxed paper on a work surface. Spoon the butter in a log shape onto the waxed paper, positioning it two-thirds of the way down from the top edge. Roll up the log in the waxed paper, then twist the ends to tighten it. Place in the refrigerator to set for about 30 minutes.

Remove the butter from the refrigerator, unwrap, and transfer to a plate for serving. Prepare the EGG to cook direct at 350°F. Take the corn out of the water and place it on the EGG cooking grid and cook, turning the ears occasionally, for about 30 minutes, or until the husk is well browned on all sides and the corn is tender.

Wearing a pair of heavy, heatproof gloves, peel back the husk on each ear and remove the silk. Serve with the butter.

This is an easy recipe to include here because I make it all the time for dinner. My fiancée, Sandi, loves this dish and brings asparagus home to remind me. It works with fat or skinny asparagus; the cooking time is just a little different. Just feel the spears to make sure they are tender before you take them off the EGG. The perforated grill wok is my preferred way to cook the asparagus, but in a pinch, you can do it right on the grill. Just make sure the spears are heading in a different direction than the slots in the cooking grid. You can reuse the marinade as a sauce here because fresh vegetables aren't a food safety hazard.

Sandi's Fave
MAKES 4 SERVINGS # Grilled Asparagus

Break off the woody ends of the asparagus and discard them. Place the spears in a shallow, flat pan. In a small bowl, whisk together the oil, vinegar, soy sauce, pepper, and granulated onion and garlic. Pour the oil mixture over the asparagus and toss to coat evenly. Marinate the asparagus at room temperature for 30 to 60 minutes, tossing occasionally.

Prepare the EGG to cook direct at 450°F. Preheat a perforated grill wok on the grill grid of the EGG. With tongs, transfer the asparagus to the wok, leaving any marinade in the pan. Cook the asparagus, tossing it occasionally, until soft and golden brown. This will take 8 to 12 minutes, depending on the size of the asparagus and how tender you like the spears.

Return the asparagus to the original pan, toss with the reserved marinade, and serve.

1 pound asparagus

⅓ cup olive oil

2 tablespoons balsamic vinegar

1 tablespoon soy sauce

½ teaspoon black pepper

½ teaspoon granulated onion

½ teaspoon granulated garlic

Chapter 4

Smoking

Smoking is probably the second-oldest cooking method known to man after grilling. Once man got tired of charring the meat directly over the fire at every meal, he raised it up or moved it to the side and discovered indirect cooking. All he had to cook with was wood, so smoking was invented. That's what smoking is: cooking indirect with a wood fire. It's not about inundating the food with smoke, however. Just because a little smoke is good, don't assume that a lot of smoke is better. Moderation is our friend in this case. You also need to know that smoke can flavor the meat without seeing a big cloud of it. A clean-burning, established fire like the EGG produces will not create a constant plume of smoke. Thin blue smoke is what you want to see.

Indirect cooking can be done in a number of ways. You can put the fire off to the side, you can put the fire really far below, or you can place a barrier between the fire and the food. The last is the way it works on the EGG, and it's by far the most efficient.

The EGG converts from a grill to a smoker-oven with the simple addition of the convEGGtor. To keep mine clean, I like to cover it with aluminum foil before I cook, but not everyone does. I also like to add a drip pan to keep the fat from dripping down into the coals.

Lump charcoal, which is charred wood, offers some wood flavor, but for smoking, you will want to add additional unburned wood. For me, a couple of chunks that add up to about the size of my fist are enough for anything. Only experience will tell you if you like a little more or a little less, but most people don't like heavy smoke on their food. Although I've suggested wood pairings in all of the recipes, feel free to use your favorite.

The recipes here all use a method that I would call hot smoking or simply barbecue. It's done by cooking indirect at a cooking temperature of 225°F to 350°F. Cold smoking, which I haven't covered here, is a method of flavoring and preserving meat without cooking it and is typically done at temperatures below 90°F. The recipes here run the gamut from the traditional barbecue staples of ribs, pork butt, brisket, and turkey to some new and out-of-the-box dishes like Chorizo and Shrimpo Fundido and Dr. BBQ's Smoked Meatball Gumbo. A little smoke flavor can enhance many oven-cooked dishes, and the EGG is the perfect vehicle for transforming them. From now on, every time you try a dish that's cooked in the oven you'll ask yourself if it would be a little better if you smoked it. Well, there's only one way to find out. Get smoking!

Smoked fish spread is something I have really come to enjoy since moving to Florida. For obvious reasons, it's a regional specialty here, typically made with smoked mullet or amberjack. You may have a hard time finding those, so look for something firm and white that's local, and if all else fails, try making the spread with catfish. Some folks add black olives; others folks leave out the jalapeños or add more of them. You really can't go wrong as long as you add enough fresh EGG-smoked fish.

Florida-Style Smoked Fish Spread MAKES ABOUT 8 SERVINGS

1 pound amberjack or other firm, white fish fillet

Kosher salt and black pepper

1 pound cream cheese, at room temperature

2 cups mayonnaise

½ medium red onion, finely chopped, plus more for garnish (optional)

2 stalks celery, finely chopped

2 jalapeño chiles, seeded and finely chopped

Finely grated zest of 1 lemon

2 tablespoons Louisiana-style hot sauce

Crackers, celery sticks, and more hot sauce, for serving

Prepare the EGG to cook indirect with a drip pan at 300°F with pecan wood added for smoke flavor. Spray a perforated grid with vegetable cooking spray. Season the fish with salt and pepper and place it on the prepared grid. Place the grid in the EGG and cook the fish until it is firm to the touch and golden brown, about 1 hour. The fish may seem a little overdone, but I find that it's better that way. It's firmer and stays chunky in the dip.

Transfer the fish to a plate and let cool for at least 30 minutes. (The fish can be smoked a day ahead, then covered and refrigerated overnight.)

In a large bowl, combine the cream cheese and mayonnaise and mix together until any lumps are gone. Add the onion, celery, chiles, lemon zest, hot sauce, and ¼ teaspoon pepper and mix until evenly incorporated. Break the fish into small pieces, discarding any errant bones, and add the pieces to the bowl. Mix gently until the fish is incorporated. Check for salt and pepper and add if needed.

Transfer to a serving bowl and garnish with additional red onion if desired. Serve with crackers, celery sticks, and hot sauce.

Deviled eggs are trendy these days, but frankly, they've been trendy at my house for as long as I can remember. They're the perfect tasty two-bite appetizer, and while they're good when plain, they can be great with some added flavors. In this case, a little smoke flavor on the whites really kicks them up. I find that to be enough smoke, and it keeps the yolk filling looking fresh and nice. If you've got grandma's recipe, try using that with the smoked yolks, too.

Smoke-Kissed Deviled Eggs

MAKES 12 SERVINGS

Place the eggs in a medium saucepan and add water to cover by 1 inch. Place over medium heat on the stove and bring the water to a boil. Remove from the heat, cover, and let rest for 12 minutes. Transfer the eggs to a colander and run cold water over them for 1 to 2 minutes, until cool. This will stop the cooking process.

Prepare the EGG to cook indirect with a drip pan at 275°F with pecan wood added for smoke flavor. Peel the eggs. Cut in half lengthwise and place the yolks in a medium bowl. Spray a perforated grid with vegetable cooking spray and lay the whites on the prepared grid. Place the perforated grid in the EGG and cook for 20 minutes.

Meanwhile, mash the yolks well with a fork. Add the mayonnaise, barbecue sauce, Sriracha sauce, granulated onion, and pepper to the yolks. Finely chop 3 of the bacon slices and add them to the yolks. Using a big spoon, mix the yolk mixture until all of the ingredients are evenly distributed and the mixture is smooth. Taste for salt and add if needed.

When the egg whites are done, transfer them, hollow side up, to a plate. Spoon the yolk mixture into a piping bag fitted with a large star or plain tip or into a resealable plastic bag with a corner cut off. Pipe the yolk mixture into the egg whites. Break the remaining bacon slice into 12 equal pieces and decorate the filling in each egg half with 1 piece, standing it up like a sail.

6 large eggs

3 tablespoons mayonnaise

1 tablespoon sweet red barbecue sauce

2 teaspoons Sriracha sauce

½ teaspoon granulated onion

¼ teaspoon black pepper

4 slices bacon, cooked, divided

Hummus is a dip made of puréed chickpeas and garlic, with other things added for flavor. Tahini, a sesame seed paste that you'll find in the international aisle at most supermarkets, is typically included. I find the whole thing kind of bland, however, so adding jalapeños and a little smoke flavor is a great solution and really sets this version apart from the usual hummus. Pita chips are the norm, and they work well, but you might also try dipping pretzel rods.

Smoked Jalapeño Hummus MAKES 6 SERVINGS

3 cloves garlic, halved lengthwise

2 jalapeño chiles, halved lengthwise

1 (15-ounce) can chickpeas, drained and rinsed

5 tablespoons olive oil, divided, plus more if needed

Juice of ½ lime

¼ cup tahini

2 tablespoons chopped fresh mint leaves, plus more for garnish

½ teaspoon kosher salt

¼ teaspoon black pepper

¼ teaspoon ground cumin

Pita chips, for serving

Prepare the EGG to cook indirect with a drip pan at 250°F with pecan wood added for smoke flavor. Cut the garlic cloves and the chiles in half lengthwise. Spray a perforated grid with vegetable cooking spray and place the garlic and chiles on the prepared grid. Place the grid in the EGG and smoke for 15 minutes. Add the chickpeas to the perforated grid and cook for another 15 minutes. Remove the grid from the EGG and set aside until all of the ingredients have cooled.

In a food processor fitted with the metal blade, combine the chiles, garlic, 4 tablespoons of the oil, the lime juice, the tahini, 2 tablespoons mint, salt, pepper, and cumin. Process for about 20 seconds, stopping and scraping down the sides of the bowl as needed, until the garlic and chiles are minced. Add the peas and process, stopping and scraping down the sides of the bowl as needed, for about 30 seconds, or until the hummus has a smooth but grainy consistency. If it's too thick, add 1 to 2 more tablespoons oil.

Transfer the hummus to a serving bowl and smooth the surface. Drizzle the remaining 1 tablespoon oil over the top. Garnish with a little mint and serve with pita chips.

Although I know this isn't very original, it just seems like some things have to be included if you're going to write a Big Green Egg cookbook: ribs, brisket, pizza, and, of course, atomic buffalo turds. This is a family book, so I'll call them poppers, but everyone likes them no matter the name or the filling. As long as you include the jalapeño and bacon and slow cook them on the EGG, they're gonna be great. These are a true EGGhead classic.

Ham and Swiss Cheese Poppers

MAKES 4 SERVINGS

Prepare the EGG to cook indirect with a drip pan at 325°F with apple wood added for smoke flavor. Cut the stem end off of each chile and, using the handle of a teaspoon, clean out and discard the ribs and seeds. Put 1 cheese stick and 1 ham stick into each chile, smashing them a bit to fit if necessary.

Starting at the tip of a chile, wrap 1 bacon slice around the chile in a spiral pattern, finishing by laying the end of the slice over the top of the chile to hold in the ham and cheese. Secure the bacon in place with a toothpick. Repeat with the remaining chiles and bacon slices.

Place the poppers, toothpick side up, on the EGG cooking grid and cook until the bacon is fully cooked and as crispy as you desire, 1 to 1½ hours.

Transfer the poppers to a platter and locate and discard all of the toothpicks before serving.

12 large jalapeño chiles

12 Swiss cheese sticks, about ¼ inch wide and thick and 1½ inches long

12 ham sticks, about ¼ inch wide and thick and 1½ inches long

12 slices bacon (not thick cut)

I'm a sucker for any dish that looks like a bowl of gooey cheese, so this was an easy recipe for me to envision. The idea was born while I was eating a shrimp and chorizo taco at a local taco stand. The combination of spicy chorizo, sweet shrimp, and a little bit of smoke is great. Chorizo comes in many variations, so look around and ask the grocer. For this dish, I used the dried (cured) chorizo, which has the look and texture of stick pepperoni, but you may find a fresh sausage and a loose spicy version in a tube, both of which are also called chorizo. All three are excellent products and would probably work in this dish.

Chorizo and Shrimpo Fundido

MAKES 10 SERVINGS

Prepare the EGG to cook indirect with a drip pan at 375°F with apple wood added for smoke flavor. Place a cast-iron Dutch oven in the EGG to preheat for 10 minutes. Add the oil to the Dutch oven and heat for 3 minutes. Add the chorizo, stir, and cook for 3 minutes. Add the shrimp, stir, and cook, stirring occasionally, for about 5 minutes, or until the shrimp begin to turn opaque.

Add the tomatoes, garlic, chile, and all but a small spoonful of the green parts of the green onions. Mix well and cook for 3 minutes. Sprinkle the flour evenly over the top, stir well, and cook, stirring occasionally, for 3 minutes, until the flour is fully incorporated and everything is hot. Add the milk, stir well, and cook, stirring occasionally, for 10 to 12 minutes, until the sauce is bubbly and begins to thicken. Add the cheese, stir to mix, and cook for 3 minutes. Stir again to blend the cheese into the sauce, cover, and cook for 5 minutes. Stir once again until mixed well, sprinkle the top with a light dusting of paprika, and cook, undisturbed, for 15 minutes, or until golden brown on top.

Garnish with the reserved green onions and serve with tortilla chips.

¼ cup olive oil

1 cup chopped dried (cured) chorizo

1 pound shrimp (26/30), peeled, deveined, and coarsely chopped

2 Roma tomatoes, seeded and diced

2 cloves garlic, crushed

1 large serrano chile, seeded and finely chopped

3 green onions, white and firm green parts, thinly sliced

¼ cup all-purpose flour

2 cups milk

1 pound Monterey Jack cheese, grated

Paprika, for dusting

Tortilla chips, for serving

Almonds, like most nuts, are high in fat, and that makes them a good candidate for the smoker. A little cooking will firm them up, but they never get dry, and they carry the smoke taste really well. It's tricky to get the seasoning to stick to nuts, however, so I add the spices to a honey mixture and let them soak in it for a bit to help out. The result is something you'll be very happy to serve and better than any nuts you will be able to buy. These aren't too spicy, so if you prefer them a little hotter, just add a little more cayenne or maybe some ground chipotle chile.

Smokin' Almonds MAKES ABOUT 8 SERVINGS

2 tablespoons honey

1 tablespoon soy sauce

1 tablespoon water

2 teaspoons chili powder

1 teaspoon noniodized table salt

¼ teaspoon dry mustard

¼ teaspoon black pepper

¼ teaspoon cayenne pepper

2 cups raw almonds

Prepare the EGG to cook indirect at 275°F with hickory wood added for smoke flavor. In a medium bowl, combine the honey, soy sauce, water, chili powder, salt, mustard, black pepper, and cayenne pepper and mix well. Add the almonds and mix to coat evenly. Let rest for 15 minutes, stirring once at the halfway point.

Spray a perforated grid with vegetable cooking spray. Spread the almonds in a single layer on the prepared grid. Place the grid in the EGG and cook for 15 minutes. Using a spatula, mix the almonds around on the grid and then settle them back into a single layer. Cook the almonds for another 15 minutes, or until they are deep brown.

Remove the grid from the EGG and immediately transfer the almonds to a sheet pan. Let cool for 15 minutes. Eat immediately or store in an airtight container at room temperature for up to a few days.

White beans make a great base for a boldly flavored one-pot dish. I've paired them with many things over the years, but in this case I've used two types of turkey, some kale, and a little bit of smoke flavor from the EGG. The outcome is something like a kicked-up version of the classic beanie weenies that we all grew up on. You can substitute more traditional pork products if you must, but I am a turkey fan.

Smoked White Beans with Turkey and Kale

MAKES ABOUT 8 SERVINGS

The night before you plan to cook, pick over beans, rinse well, then place in a large glass bowl and add cold water to cover by 3 inches. Cover the bowl with plastic wrap and let stand at room temperature for 12 hours or so.

Prepare the EGG to cook indirect with a drip pan at 375°F with pecan wood added for smoke flavor. Place a cast-iron Dutch oven on the EGG cooking grid and preheat for 10 minutes. Add the oil, kielbasa, necks, and onion to the Dutch oven, stir to coat everything with the oil, and cook for 1 hour, stirring occasionally. Drain the beans, add them to the pot along with the broth, water, garlic, pepper, and kale, and mix gently until everything is evenly blended. Cook for 1 hour, stirring occasionally. Place the cover on the Dutch oven and cook for 1 hour more, stirring once at the halfway point. Add additional water if the beans become dry. They should always be just submerged in broth but not as much as a soup. Uncover the pot and test the beans for doneness. They should be very tender. If they aren't, re-cover and continue cooking in the closed EGG until they are.

Remove the Dutch oven from the EGG, then remove the turkey necks from the pot and let cool for 10 minutes. Using your hands, pull the meat from the necks and shred it. Return the meat to the pot and discard the bones. Mix well and serve.

1 pound (about 2 cups) dried great Northern beans

¼ cup olive oil

1 pound smoked turkey kielbasa, sliced on the diagonal ½ inch thick

1 pound smoked turkey necks, cut into 3 or 4 pieces total

1 medium red onion, finely chopped

4 cups vegetable broth

3 cups water

2 cloves garlic, crushed

½ teaspoon black pepper

3 cups chopped kale

This is pulled beef, named because you simply pull the meat into strands after you've cooked it into submission. It starts with a simple chuck roast, which is smoked first for flavor and caramelization and then covered with some liquid in a pan to get it tender. When it's all done, it has cooked down to a beautiful soft and tasty product that's perfect for making sammiches, which are kind of like sloppy joes. With a little creativity, this could evolve into some *buenos* tacos or burritos, too.

Barbecue Beef Sammiches MAKES ABOUT 10 SAMMICHES

4 pounds boneless beef chuck roast

RUB

1 tablespoon kosher salt

1 tablespoon paprika

1 tablespoon chili powder

1 tablespoon granulated onion

1 tablespoon granulated garlic

1 tablespoon granulated sugar

2 teaspoons black pepper

SAUCE

1 cup beef broth

½ cup ketchup

¼ cup firmly packed light brown sugar

¼ cup cider vinegar

1 tablespoon soy sauce

1 teaspoon kosher salt

1 teaspoon chili powder

1 teaspoon granulated garlic

½ teaspoon cayenne pepper

1 large red onion, chopped

10 fluffy white hamburger buns

Prepare the EGG to cook indirect with a drip pan at 350°F with cherry wood added for smoke flavor. To make the rub, combine all of the ingredients in a small bowl and mix well. Cut the meat into 4 equal pieces. Season the pieces on all sides with the rub, using it all. Place the meat on the EGG cooking grid and cook for 1 hour.

Meanwhile, make the sauce. Combine all of the ingredients in a large bowl and mix well. Set aside.

After the beef has cooked for 1 hour, transfer it to a disposable aluminum foil pan. Pour the sauce over the top and cover the pan with foil, sealing it tightly. Place the pan in the EGG and cook for 2 hours, or until the beef is falling-apart tender. Peek under the foil after 1 hour to check the level of the liquid. There should be about 1 inch of liquid in the bottom of the pan. If there isn't, just add a little more beef broth or water.

When the meat is done, transfer it to a sheet pan, reserving the juices in the foil pan. In about 15 minutes, the beef should be cool enough to handle. Using your hands, shred the meat into strands, discarding any remaining big pieces of fat. Return the meat to the foil pan and mix it with the juices. It should now be the proper consistency to make sammiches. If the meat needs a little more liquid, add a small amount of beef broth or water. Using tongs, load up the buns with meat to serve.

A big pot of red chili is a great dish for a large gathering of friends, and it's never better than when it's cooked over a fire. The beef is smoked for an added dimension that works well with the spicy broth, and then the whole pot is cooked on the EGG to make sure the broth gets some good wood flavor, as well. I like to serve this chili with cooked macaroni, grated cheese, raw onions, and oyster crackers.

Chunky Chili con Carne MAKES ABOUT 10 SERVINGS

6 dried California chiles

4 cups beef broth, divided

3 pounds boneless beef chuck, cut into 1-inch cubes

1 teaspoon kosher salt, plus more for seasoning meat

Black pepper

¼ cup olive oil

1 large yellow onion, chopped

1 large green bell pepper, seeded and chopped

3 stalks celery, chopped

2 jalapeño chiles, chopped

2 tablespoons ground cumin

¼ cup chili powder

½ teaspoon cayenne pepper

2 cups canned diced tomatoes, with juices

2 to 3 cups water, divided

1 (16-ounce) can light red kidney beans, drained and rinsed

1 (16-ounce) can dark red kidney beans, drained and rinsed

Favorite condiments, for serving

Prepare the EGG to cook indirect with a drip pan at 300°F with apple wood added for smoke flavor. Place the chiles in a medium bowl and pour 2 cups of the broth over them. Set aside to rehydrate.

Season the meat with salt and black pepper. Spray a large perforated grid with vegetable cooking spray. Spread the meat in a single layer on the prepared grid. Place the grid in the EGG and smoke the meat for 45 minutes, or until firm and golden brown.

Meanwhile, start the broth on the stove. Heat a cast-iron Dutch oven over medium heat and add the oil. When the oil is hot, add the onion, bell pepper, celery, and chiles and mix well. Cook, stirring occasionally, for about 8 minutes, or until the onion is tender.

Meanwhile, place the chiles and their soaking liquid in a blender and blend on high speed for about 1 minute, or until completely puréed, then reserve. When the onion-celery mixture is ready, add the cumin, chili powder, the remaining 1 teaspoon salt, and the cayenne pepper. Mix well and cook for 1 minute to toast the spices. Add the tomatoes and mix well. Add the chile mixture, water, and the remaining 2 cups broth. Bring to a simmer, stirring occasionally.

When the meat is done, raise the temperature of the EGG to 325°F. Add the meat to the broth mixture and stir well. Transfer the Dutch oven to the EGG and cook the chili, uncovered, for 1 hour. Mix well and add the beans. Cover the Dutch oven and then continue cooking for 1 hour. Stir the chili and add the remaining 1 cup water if the mixture seems too dry, keeping in mind that this is a thick and chunky chili. Cover the pot and then the EGG and continue cooking until the meat is very tender. This should take another 30 to 60 minutes.

Stir the chili and taste for salt, adding some if needed. Serve with your favorite condiments.

This is one of those ideas that I've had for a long time, and I'm really happy to get around to sharing it finally. Gumbo by nature is a catchall dish that uses what you have. The gravy is key and must be made with a roux and the trinity of onion, celery, and bell pepper, but beyond that, anything goes. Meatballs seemed like a good addition, and after eating this, I think you'll agree that they are. Filé powder is a common gumbo ingredient. It's made by grinding sassafras leaves and is used to thicken the sauce and add a little earthy flavor. This gumbo is best served with plenty of white rice, hot sauce, and cold beer.

Dr. BBQ's Smoked Meatball Gumbo

MAKES ABOUT 8 SERVINGS

MEATBALLS

12 ounces ground beef

12 ounces ground pork

2 large eggs, lightly beaten

1/4 cup grated Parmesan cheese

1/4 cup finely chopped fresh curly parsley

1/2 teaspoon granulated onion

1/2 teaspoon granulated garlic

1 tablespoon kosher salt

1 teaspoon black pepper

1/2 cup dried bread crumbs

GRAVY

1 cup corn oil

1 cup all-purpose flour

1 large yellow onion, cut into small dice

3 stalks celery, cut into small dice

1 medium green bell pepper, seeded and cut into small dice

1 medium red bell pepper, seeded and cut into small dice

2 cups diced andouille or smoked pork sausage (about 3/8-inch dice)

3 cloves garlic, crushed

2 jalapeño chiles, seeded, ribs removed, and minced

2 1/2 cups canned diced tomatoes, with juices

6 cups beef broth

1 tablespoon dried thyme leaves

2 teaspoons kosher salt

2 teaspoons black pepper

2 tablespoons filé powder

Cooked white rice, for serving

Hot sauce, for serving

(continued)

(continued from page 65)

Prepare the EGG to cook indirect with a drip pan at 350°F with pecan wood added for smoke flavor. To make the meatballs, in a large bowl, combine the beef and pork, break them up into small pieces, and mix well. Pour the eggs over the meat, then sprinkle the Parmesan, parsley, granulated onion and garlic, salt, and pepper evenly over the eggs. Using your hands, mix together until fully blended. Sprinkle the bread crumbs over the top and mix again until well blended. Form 16 meatballs, each about the size of a golf ball. If you're using a scale, the meatballs will weigh 2 ounces each. Spray a large perforated grid with vegetable cooking spray and place the meatballs, not touching, on the grid. Place the grid in the EGG and cook for 45 minutes.

While the meatballs are cooking, start the gravy in the kitchen. Heat a large cast-iron Dutch oven over medium heat. Add the oil and flour and mix well with a wooden spoon to create a roux. Cook, stirring constantly, until the roux is a dark chocolate brown. This will take 15 to 30 minutes, depending on your heat. Do not try to rush the process, and be careful not to burn the roux or you'll need to start all over. If you feel it's close to burning, turn down the heat. This is particularly high risk toward the end. As soon as you think the roux is dark enough, add the onion, celery, and bell peppers and continue stirring. This will cool the roux and end the risk of burning. Cook and stir for 5 minutes, or until the vegetables are soft. Add the garlic and jalapeños and stir and cook for 1 minute. Add the sausage and continue cooking and stirring for another 5 minutes. Add the tomatoes with their juices, thyme, salt, and pepper and mix well. Bring the mixture to a simmer and cook, stirring occasionally, for another 5 minutes. Add the broth, bring to a simmer, cover, and cook, stirring occasionally, for 15 minutes.

When the meatballs are done, add them to the gravy and stir well. Place the Dutch oven in the EGG, cover the Dutch oven, close the EGG lid, and cook for 30 minutes, stirring once at the halfway point. Remove the Dutch oven cover, close the EGG lid, and cook for another 30 minutes, stirring once at the halfway point.

Remove the pot from the EGG. Add the filé powder to the gumbo and stir until the sauce thickens. Serve the gumbo spooned over rice.

Turkey is the forgotten bird most of the year and that just isn't right. It's easy to cook and it's delicious. I like the white meat when it's cooked just right, so tender and juicy, but I like the dark meat, too. Turkey thighs are a meaty bargain. This brine and smoke method hits the dark-meat mark for me. I don't find a need for any sauce because the brine makes these sweet, tender, and juicy just as they are. But if you are a barbecue sauce junkie, your favorite sweet sauce is going to pair very well here.

Brined and Smoked Turkey Thighs

MAKES 4 SERVINGS

A day before you plan to cook, make the brine. Heat the cold water in a medium saucepan over medium heat. Add the salt, sugar, granulated onion, lemon pepper, allspice, sage, and nutmeg and mix well. Heat, stirring often, for 3 to 4 minutes, until the salt and sugar are incorporated. The water should be warm but not boiling. Put the slushy ice water in a large bowl. Add the hot brine and mix until the ice melts. Cover and refrigerate the brine for at least 1 hour and preferably overnight, until very cold.

Add the thighs to a large, heavy-duty resealable bag. Pour the brine over the thighs and then move the thighs around so all of the air rises to the top. Seal the bag, forcing out as much air as possible. Place the bag in a bowl in case of leaks and place the bowl in the refrigerator for 12 to 24 hours, flipping the bag and moving the thighs around once or twice.

Prepare the EGG to cook indirect with a drip pan at 325°F with apple wood added for smoke flavor. Remove the thighs from the brine, discard the brine, and rinse the thighs well. Dry the thighs well, then brush them with the olive oil, coating evenly on all sides. Place the thighs, skin side up, on the EGG cooking grid and cook for about 2 hours, or until they reach an internal temperature of 190°F deep in the meaty part.

Transfer the thighs to a platter, tent loosely with aluminum foil, and let rest for 5 minutes. Serve 1 thigh to each diner, or slice the thighs and serve them family-style.

BRINE

2 cups cold water

¼ cup kosher salt

¼ cup raw sugar

2 tablespoons granulated onion

2 teaspoons lemon pepper

1 teaspoon ground allspice

1 teaspoon rubbed sage

½ teaspoon ground nutmeg

2 cups slushy ice-cold water

4 turkey thighs, about 1 pound each

2 tablespoons olive oil

Cookie butter, aka *speculoos* spread, is a magical, tasty creation that's kind of like peanut butter that tastes like a really good cookie. It's good on toast, on a cracker, on a cookie, or on a spoon straight from the jar, so I thought I'd try making a barbecue sauce out of this amazing stuff and it worked! It's a little thick and gloppy, but the taste easily makes up for any weirdness in the texture. OK, the ribs are pretty good, too, and you could substitute your favorite barbecue sauce, but then you'd just never know what you were missing. You can find cookie butter at most supermarkets or at Trader Joe's.

Baby Back Ribs with Cookie Butter Barbecue Sauce MAKES 9 SERVINGS

RUB
¼ cup raw sugar

3 tablespoons kosher salt

3 tablespoons paprika

1 teaspoon granulated onion

1 teaspoon granulated garlic

1 teaspoon cayenne pepper

3 slabs pork loin baby back ribs, about 6 pounds total

1 cup fresh orange juice

SAUCE
1½ cups cookie butter (speculoos spread)

1½ cups ketchup

1 cup fresh orange juice

Juice of ½ lemon

2 tablespoons hot sauce

2 tablespoons paprika

2 teaspoons granulated onion

1 teaspoon granulated garlic

1 tablespoon soy sauce

½ teaspoon kosher salt

Prepare the EGG to cook indirect with a drip pan at 300°F with cherry wood added for smoke flavor.
To make the rub, combine all of the ingredients in a small bowl and mix well. Peel the membrane off the back of each slab of ribs. Season the ribs liberally on both sides with the rub, using it all. Let the ribs rest for 10 minutes, or until the rub is tacky.

Lay the slabs, meaty side up, on the EGG cooking grid and cook for 2 hours. Flip the ribs and cook for 1 hour longer, or until well browned on both sides.

Lay 3 big doubled sheets of heavy-duty aluminum foil on a work surface. Lay a rib slab, meaty side up, on the center of each doubled foil stack. Fold up the edges of each foil stack and then add ⅓ cup of the orange juice to each packet. Close up each rib packet snugly, being careful not to puncture the foil with a rib bone. Put the ribs back on the EGG and cook for 1 hour, or until tender when poked with a toothpick or fork.

Meanwhile, make the sauce. Melt the cookie butter in a medium saucepan over medium heat on the stove. Add the ketchup, orange juice, lemon juice, hot sauce, paprika, granulated onion and garlic, soy sauce, and salt. Mix well and cook, stirring often, for about 3 minutes, or until well blended. Set aside.

When the ribs are tender to your liking, remove them from the foil packets and place them, meaty side down, on the grid. Brush with a liberal coating of the sauce and cook for 15 minutes, or until the sauce is tacky. Flip the ribs and brush a liberal coating of the sauce on the meaty side and cook for 15 minutes. Brush the ribs with a second coat of the sauce and cook for 30 minutes, or until the sauce is set.

Transfer the ribs to a cutting board and cut each slab into thirds. Arrange on a platter and serve.

The reality is that in Memphis folks eat their ribs wet and dry and don't care as much about the difference as the writers who write about it from afar. But dry-rubbed ribs were definitely invented at the Rendezvous, and very good versions of them are now made all over town. The other half of this name, the St. Louis cut, isn't really a St. Louis thing at all. But no matter, as it's a good thing for us all. It calls for the best part of the sparerib, which comes from the same area on the hog as bacon. Enough said. These ribs, which are cooked with only a dry rub, are my personal favorite for eating.

Memphis Dry-Rubbed St. Louis–Style Ribs MAKES 4 TO 6 SERVINGS

RUB

¼ cup paprika

3 tablespoons raw sugar

2 tablespoons kosher salt

1 tablespoon granulated onion

1 tablespoon granulated garlic

1 teaspoon dried basil leaves

1 teaspoon cayenne pepper

2 slabs St. Louis–style pork spareribs, about 4 pounds total

½ cup apple juice

½ cup cider vinegar

Prepare the EGG to cook indirect with a drip pan at 300°F with hickory wood added for smoke flavor. To make the rub, combine all of the ingredients in a small bowl and mix well. Peel the membrane off the back of each slab of ribs. Season the ribs on both sides using about half of the rub. Let the ribs rest for 15 minutes, or until the rub is tacky.

Lay the ribs, meaty side up, on the EGG cooking grid and cook for 2 hours. Flip the ribs and cook for 1 hour longer, or until the ribs are nicely browned on both sides.

Lay 2 big doubled sheets of heavy-duty aluminum foil on a work surface. Lay a rib slab, meaty side up, on the center of each doubled foil stack. In a small bowl, stir together the apple juice and vinegar, mixing well. Fold up the edges of each foil stack and then add ¼ cup of the juice mixture to each packet. Close up each rib packet snugly, being careful not to puncture the foil with a rib bone. Reserve the remaining ½ cup juice mixture.

Put the ribs back in the EGG and cook for 1 hour, or until tender when poked with a toothpick or fork. Remove the ribs from the foil packets and place them, bone side down, on the grid. Drizzle the ribs with ⅓ cup of the reserved juice mixture and sprinkle them with some of the remaining rub. Cook for about another 15 minutes, or until the ribs are dry.

Transfer to a platter and drizzle with the remaining juice mixture. With a big knife, cut the ribs into individual bones. Serve with any remaining rub on the side.

Pork steaks, bone in and cut from the blade, are a great item for the grill or smoker. They're really just slices from a pork butt, which is about the best piece of meat you can cook. These steaks are the first thing I mastered in my early days of grilling. Back then, I just seasoned them and grilled them with a last-minute glaze of barbecue sauce, but I have since learned the ways of the grill masters who live in St. Louis, where pork steaks are king. My recipe is pretty true to tradition, but to get it just right, you'll need to find some of the hometown favorite Maull's barbecue sauce.

Tender and Tasty
Pork Steaks MAKES 4 SERVINGS

RUB

1 tablespoon kosher salt

1 tablespoon paprika

2 teaspoons black pepper

2 teaspoons granulated onion

2 teaspoons granulated garlic

4 pork blade steaks,
   about 1 inch thick

SAUCE

1½ cups sweet barbecue sauce

¼ cup apple juice

2 tablespoons Louisiana hot sauce

1 medium yellow onion,
   finely chopped

Prepare the EGG to cook indirect with a drip pan at 300°F with apple wood added for smoke flavor.

To make the rub, combine all of the ingredients in a small bowl and mix well. Season the steaks evenly on both sides with the rub, using it all.

Put the steaks on the EGG cooking grid and cook for 1 hour. Flip the steaks and cook for 1 hour more. Transfer the steaks to a disposable aluminum foil pan, arranging them so they cascade onto one another. Raise the temperature of the EGG to 350°F.

To make the sauce, combine all of the ingredients in a medium bowl and mix well. Pour the sauce over the steaks, coating them all evenly. Cover the foil pan tightly with foil, place the pan in the EGG, and cook for about 1½ hours, or until the steaks are very tender when poked with a fork.

Transfer the steaks to a platter, top with any remaining pan juices, and serve.

This is the real thing. If you want to cook a brisket, saddle up and get a big fat one and ride out the long cook. There really is nothing quite like this on the plate, and a flat cut or a piece of a brisket just won't be the same. An old barbecue man once told me that the reason he liked to cook brisket so much was because it allowed him to cook it for a long time. Shorter cooks just won't taste the same. In Texas, brisket is served with white bread, raw onions, and jalapeño chiles. A pot of real pinto beans would go nicely, too, but don't make them too sweet if you want them Texas style. Barbecue sauce would be seriously optional, and I'm in the no-sauce camp.

Texas-Style Beef Brisket

MAKES ABOUT 12 SERVINGS

Prepare the EGG to cook indirect with a drip pan at 275°F with oak wood added for smoke flavor. Using a sharp knife, trim some of the fat from between the two muscles so it will cook evenly. Leave the fat cap intact.

In a small bowl, combine the salt, pepper, and ground chipotle chile and mix well. Rub the brisket all over with the oil, then season it liberally with the rub, using it all. There's no need to season the fat cap.

Place the brisket, fat side down, on the EGG cooking grid and cook for 6 hours. Flip and cook for another 2 hours.

Lay a big doubled sheet of heavy-duty aluminum foil on a work surface. Lay the brisket, fat side up, on the foil. As you close up the foil around the brisket, pour the coffee into the package and then seal it. Return the brisket to the EGG and cook until it reaches an internal temperature of 205°F in the thickest part. This should take another 3 to 4 hours. When the brisket reaches the right temperature, transfer it to an empty ice chest and let it rest for up to 4 hours.

Take the brisket out of the ice chest. Carefully unseal the foil package and transfer the brisket to a cutting board. Pour the juices into a clear glass measuring cup. Trim away all of the excess fat from the brisket, then slice through both muscles against the grain and about ³⁄₈ inch thick. Arrange the slices on a platter. Using a spoon, remove as much fat as possible from the juices, then drizzle the juices over the brisket slices and serve.

1 (12-pound) whole beef brisket

¼ cup kosher salt

¼ cup coarsely ground black pepper

1 tablespoon ground chipotle chile

2 tablespoons olive oil

1 cup brewed coffee

I don't typically like using a cut piece of a brisket in a smoker, as it tends to dry out. But because this brisket flat is braised to finish, it's a good choice here. The meat flavors the gravy and the gravy flavors the meat and the result is amazing. Use whatever dried red chiles you can find or have around. I like the California-ancho combination, but plenty of other good ones are possible. This meat and the gravy would make a great beginning for a tamale party or a pan of enchiladas, but I like it simply sliced with some white rice.

Red Chile Brisket MAKES ABOUT 6 SERVINGS

RUB

1 tablespoon kosher salt

1 teaspoon black pepper

1 teaspoon chili powder

1 (3½-pound) piece brisket flat, with ¼-inch-thick fat cap

RED CHILE SAUCE

3 dried California chiles

3 ancho chiles

3 cups beef broth

6 green onions, white and firm green parts, coarsely chopped

2 cloves garlic, crushed

2 chipotle chiles in adobo sauce

2 tablespoons all-purpose flour

½ teaspoon kosher salt

½ teaspoon ground cumin

½ teaspoon dried oregano leaves

Cooked white rice, for serving

Prepare the EGG to cook indirect with a drip pan at 300°F with hickory wood added for smoke flavor. To make the rub, combine all of the ingredients in a small bowl and mix well. Season the brisket evenly on all sides with the rub, using it all. Let the brisket rest for 15 minutes, or until the rub is tacky.

Place the brisket, fat side down, on the EGG cooking grid and cook for 3 hours.

Meanwhile, make the sauce. Cut the stems off of the California and ancho chiles, then place the chiles in a glass bowl. Add the broth and let soak for 1 to 2 hours. Transfer the chiles and broth to a blender and add the green onions, garlic, chipotle chiles, flour, salt, cumin, and oregano. Blend on low speed for 15 seconds and then on high speed for 30 seconds, or until puréed. Set aside.

After the brisket has cooked for 3 hours, transfer it, fat side down, to an EGG-safe 9 by 13-inch pan. Pour the chile mixture over the brisket, then place the pan back in the EGG. Raise the temperature of the EGG to 325°F and cook for 1 hour. Flip the brisket and cover the pan tightly with aluminum foil. Cook for about 1 hour longer, or until the brisket reaches an internal temperature of 205°F and is tender.

Remove the pan from the EGG and let the brisket rest for 15 minutes. Transfer the brisket to a cutting board and thinly slice against the grain. Serve with rice and with the pan juices as a sauce.

Smoked food doesn't have to be the same old things. That great wood flavor works on traditional stovetop dishes, too, like beef and noodles. Just leave the lid off the pot and stir it up once in a while and you'll have smoked gravy, as well. I cheated and started the gravy on the stove while the beef was smoking, but you can wait until it's done and cook the whole dish on the EGG if you like. I call for stew meat here. That just means beef cut into bite-size cubes. You can buy it already cut up or buy a chuck roast and cut it up yourself.

Beef Tips in Double Onion Gravy

MAKES 8 SERVINGS

Prepare the EGG to cook indirect with a drip pan at 325°F with cherry wood added for smoke flavor. Season the meat with salt and pepper. Spray a perforated grid with cooking spray. Spread the meat on the prepared grid. Place the grid in the EGG and cook for 45 minutes, or until golden brown.

Meanwhile, in the kitchen, heat the oil in a large Dutch oven over medium heat on the stove. Add both onions and cook, stirring occasionally, for about 5 minutes. Add the garlic and mushrooms, stir to mix, and cook, stirring occasionally, for another 3 to 4 minutes, until the mushrooms are soft. Sprinkle the flour evenly over the onion mixture, mix it in, and then cook, stirring often, for 1 to 2 minutes, until the flour is fully incorporated. Add 2 cups of the broth, the soy sauce, Worcestershire sauce, the 1 teaspoon black pepper, and marjoram and bring to a simmer, stirring occasionally. Add the remaining 3 cups broth and return the mixture to a simmer, stirring occasionally.

When the beef is ready, add it to the Dutch oven, stir, and cover. Place the Dutch oven in the EGG and cook for 1 hour, stirring at the halfway point. After 1 hour, stir again and cook for 1 hour more, stirring at the halfway point. Uncover the Dutch oven, stir, and check the meat for tenderness. If it is not tender, re-cover and keep cooking, checking every 30 minutes, until the meat is very tender.

When the meat is ready, taste the gravy and add salt if needed. Serve over noodles.

3 pounds boneless stew beef, cut into bite-size pieces

Kosher salt

1 teaspoon black pepper, plus more for seasoning meat

¼ cup olive oil

1 medium red onion, finely chopped

1 medium white onion, finely chopped

4 cloves garlic, crushed

8 ounces baby bella (crimini) mushrooms, thinly sliced

⅓ cup all-purpose flour

5 cups beef broth, divided

¼ cup soy sauce

1 tablespoon Worcestershire sauce

1½ teaspoons dried marjoram leaves

Cooked flat noodles, for serving

Salmon is one of those distinct tastes that many people really love. Torie, our neighbor, is a huge fan and is very happy whenever I am testing salmon recipes. Salmon takes well to many different flavors, but a little smoke seems to be the favorite. Here, I use a quick brine for flavor and moistness and a sweet brown sugar topping. This is considered hot smoking. It's a close relative of the cured and cold smoked salmon that you pair with bagels, but this one is best enjoyed fresh and hot.

MAKES 2 SERVINGS EGG Smoked Salmon

At least 4 hours before you plan to cook, make the brine. In a microwave-safe bowl, combine the cold water, salt, sugar, lemon pepper, and allspice and mix well. Microwave on high for 1 minute and then stir until blended. Add the slushy ice water and mix until the ice is melted. Cover and refrigerate for at least 1 hour and preferably overnight, until very cold.

Place the salmon in a heavy-duty resealable bag. Pour the cold brine over the salmon and seal the bag, forcing out as much air as possible. Place the bag in a bowl in case of leaks and place the bowl in the refrigerator for 3 hours, flipping the bag occasionally.

Prepare the EGG to cook indirect with a drip pan at 300°F with pecan wood added for smoke flavor. Remove the salmon from the brine, discard the brine, and rinse the salmon well under cold running water. Dry the salmon well. Spray a perforated grid with vegetable cooking spray and place the salmon on the prepared grid. Top each piece of salmon with half of the brown sugar, spreading it evenly.

Place the grid in the EGG and cook the salmon until firm to the touch and you just barely begin to see the white fat bubble up from it. This should take, depending on the thickness of the salmon, between 30 and 40 minutes.

Remove the salmon from the EGG and serve immediately.

BRINE

1 cup cold water

2 tablespoons Morton brand coarse kosher salt

2 tablespoons raw sugar

1 teaspoon lemon pepper

¼ teaspoon ground allspice

1 cup slushy ice-cold water

2 (6-ounce) salmon fillets

¼ cup firmly packed light brown sugar

A pork butt is the ultimate piece of barbecue meat. It combines tasty pork and the fat that will baste it as it slowly cooks into a luscious, melting pile of deliciousness, with a crusty, smoky bark on the outside. And no place loves this type of pork more than North Carolina. But there are two sides of the state. In the eastern part, folks like a very tangy, almost-straight-up vinegar sauce, and in the western part of the state, a little bit of ketchup is added to the sauce for sweetness. Both are tasty, but if I had to pick one, I'd choose the western style. So here it is.

Barbecued Pork Shoulder with Carolina Sauce MAKES ABOUT 12 SERVINGS

1 (8-pound) whole bone-in pork butt

2 tablespoons olive oil

RUB

2 tablespoons kosher salt

2 tablespoons black pepper

2 tablespoons paprika

1 tablespoon granulated garlic

½ cup apple juice

SAUCE

1 cup cider vinegar

½ cup ketchup

1 tablespoon firmly packed light brown sugar

1 teaspoon kosher salt

1 teaspoon Worcestershire

½ teaspoon red pepper flakes

Prepare the EGG to cook indirect with a drip pan at 275°F with hickory wood added for smoke flavor. Trim off any loose fat from the butt but leave the heavy fat cap intact. Rub the butt all over with the oil. To make the rub, combine all of the ingredients in a small bowl and mix well. Season the butt liberally on all of the meaty surfaces with the rub, using it all. There's no need to season the fat cap.

Place the butt, fat side down, on the EGG cooking grid and cook for about 8 hours, or until it reaches an internal temperature of 170°F.

Lay a big doubled sheet of heavy-duty aluminum foil on a work surface. Lay the pork butt, fat side up, in the center of the doubled foil. As you begin to close up the foil around the butt, pour the apple juice into the bottom of the package and then seal the package. Put the butt back in the EGG and cook until it reaches an internal temperature of 200°F deep in the meaty part. This should take another 2 to 3 hours.

Meanwhile, make the sauce. Combine all of the ingredients in a medium saucepan over medium heat on the stove and mix well. Cook, stirring often, for about 8 minutes, or until the sauce begins to simmer. Remove from the heat and set aside.

When the pork is done, remove it from the EGG and open the package. Let cool for 15 minutes. Wearing a pair of heavy, heatproof gloves or using tongs, pull the pork apart, discarding any fat or bones. Once the pork has been pulled apart, place it on a cutting board and chop with a cleaver or large knife. In North Carolina, cooks chop it pretty small. I like it a little chunkier. Place the pork in a large pan or bowl, top it with half of the sauce, and toss to combine. Serve with the remaining sauce on the side.

Chapter 5

Baking

Baking is something that everyone does at home in the oven, but baking on the EGG is way more fun, and it helps keep the house cool on hot days. It also adds a little taste of the outdoors to your dishes, which sets them apart from average fare. Baking is defined as cooking in an enclosed space using consistent indirect dry heat. It is commonly used and associated with breads, cakes, pies, and cookies. Pizza is really just a flat bread with toppings, so it's baked as well. In the home kitchen, casseroles, potatoes, and other one-pan dishes are also baked. Commonly used baking temperatures are between 350°F and 400°F. Cooking indirect at these temperatures is a simple accomplishment on the EGG. Just use the indirect setup with a full load of charcoal and bring your EGG to the desired temperature using the start-up method described in chapter 2 (page 8).

Here are some things to consider before you start that are unique to baking in the EGG. First, what are you cooking and what did you last cook in your EGG? If the answers are a cake and chicken wings, you are going to want to change out any lumps of charcoal that look like they have food drippings on them or your cake will pick up that leftover chicken-wing taste. Just take out the old charcoal before lighting and set it aside to be used later when you're cooking something more chicken fat–friendly. Fill 'er up with some clean new charcoal and you are ready to roll. It's also important to have your EGG up to temperature

and fully stabilized before baking, so start your fire a bit early. This will ensure that you get only the good wood-oven taste while avoiding the extra smokiness of start-up. If you have an electronic temperature control device, this is a good time to use it. Seriously consistent temperature is a good thing when baking.

A couple of other commonsense ideas when baking in the EGG are to use a cooking vessel that's friendly to the round shape. Obviously a round cake pan or a pizza pan is a good idea, but when that isn't possible, try to use a square one. Oval and rectangular are the least desirable shapes for consistent cooking. Just use the old "spin it around" technique, and you should be fine. That's when you rotate the pan one-third or one-half of a turn every 15 or 20 minutes. This will solve all uneven cooking when you are baking in the EGG and also any problems that may occur if the cooking grid isn't perfectly level.

I don't care for any added wood flavor when baking, but some of you smoke eaters may like a little. Please use something mild like apple or cherry wood if you must. Last but not least, I want to encourage you to try any and all of your favorite baking recipes on the EGG. Just use the same lid temperature as you would for your oven and check for doneness with a thermometer or a toothpick, because the timing may need to be adjusted. Once you master baking in the EGG, you may never use your oven again!

The Big Green Egg is a truly versatile and fun piece of cooking equipment. Your friends and family will be amazed when you fire it up in the morning to make a great make-ahead breakfast. I like blueberries, and they were beautiful the day I made this for the first time, so they are in the recipe. But if they don't look good that day or you like strawberries better, go for it. Even bananas or peaches would work. Just be sure the casserole gets cooked in the middle and it will be great.

Blueberry French Toast Casserole MAKES ABOUT 8 SERVINGS

15 slices Texas toast–style white bread

1 pound breakfast sausage, cooked, crumbled, and cooled

8 large eggs

2 cups half-and-half

1 cup milk

2 tablespoons firmly packed light brown sugar

1 tablespoon vanilla extract

½ teaspoon kosher salt

½ cup salted butter, melted and cooled

4 ounces fresh blueberries

Maple syrup, warmed, for serving

The night before you plan to cook, tear each bread slice into 9 pieces and put the pieces in a large bowl. Add the sausage and toss to mix. In another large bowl, beat the eggs until frothy and blended. Add the half-and-half, milk, sugar, vanilla, and salt and whisk until well blended. Add the butter and whisk until blended. Pour the egg mixture over the bread mixture. Using a large spoon, gently fold them together until the bread is evenly soaked.

Spray a 9 by 13-inch EGG-safe pan with vegetable cooking spray. Pour the bread mixture into the pan and spread it evenly. Sprinkle the blueberries over the top, distributing them evenly, and then push them down into the bread mixture just to hold them in place. Cover the casserole and refrigerate for at least 4 hours and up to 24 hours.

In the morning, take the casserole out of the refrigerator to warm at room temperature for 1 hour. Prepare the EGG to cook indirect at 350°F. Uncover the casserole, place it on the EGG cooking grid, and cook for 30 minutes. Spin the casserole 180 degrees to ensure even cooking and continue cooking for another 25 to 30 minutes, until the casserole is firm and set in the middle.

Remove from the EGG and let rest for 5 minutes. Serve with maple syrup on the side.

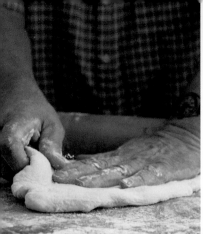

PIZZA

Baking pizza in an EGG makes great pizzas at home! The next eight recipes are all about pizza. It's fairly easy to cook pizza on the EGG, but it is a complex subject. You can simply cook a frozen or premade pizza on a pizza stone on your EGG and it will be darn good. Or you can make the pizza from scratch and it will be even better.

For any good pizza, you need to start with good dough. You can buy fresh dough at many supermarkets or from a local pizzeria, but I wanted to make fresh dough, and once I did, it was my favorite. It's not hard to make. You'll need a kitchen scale to weigh the flour, and you'll need to make it a day or two ahead of time. Because it's critical to weigh the flour for good pizza dough, I have not included volume measurements for the flour in the two dough recipes that follow.

Ginny and Kim Youngblood are longtime EGGheads and friends. They're also pizza aficionados, so I figured I'd start with them for advice. Ginny and Kim teach pizza classes at the Big Green Egg Culinary Center in Atlanta and at other EGG dealers and EGGfests around the country. They offered to share their recipes for two kinds of crust, pizza sauce, and even a dessert pizza. Those recipes are all here, with only a few editorial adaptations. They also helped me a lot with techniques and with the way they make their pizzas. I enlisted the help of Big Green Egg Interactive Communications Manager Rob D'Amico, as well. Rob, aka Guido, is a serious pizza enthusiast, and he helped me by passing along his cooking technique and some calzone tips. Rob also suggested using parchment paper under the pizzas, which I think is a great idea. It makes them easy to handle yet allows the stone to make the crust crispy.

So armed with all that help and a lifetime of pizza-eating experience, I offer the recipes that follow. Each has its own story and style, but they are all well worth the effort.

This is a really good recipe for thin-crust pizza. I use it for pizzas, garlic knots, and calzones. A kitchen scale and good-quality bread flour are critical to success. I bought King Arthur's bread flour online but later saw it at a local supermarket. Once this dough had rested for two to three days, it was easy to roll out. Like any dough, do not overwork it or add too much extra flour. Roll it quickly, top it, and cook it.

Ginny and Kim's Thin-Crust Pizza Dough

MAKES DOUGH FOR FOUR 14-INCH PIZZAS

In the bowl of a stand mixer, combine the flour, salt, and yeast. Stir to mix well and let stand. Attach the dough hook and mix on low speed for 3 minutes, scraping down the sides occasionally. Turn off the mixer and let the mixture rest for 5 to 10 minutes to allow the yeast to combine with the flour. Restart the mixer on low speed and add the sugar. Slowly pour in the water while the mixer is running. Add the 2 tablespoons oil and continue mixing on low speed for 4 to 5 minutes, until the dough is well blended, has a smooth appearance, and has come together into a ball. If the dough won't all come together or it's too dry, add additional water, 1 tablespoon at a time. If the dough is too sticky, add additional flour, 1 tablespoon at a time.

Transfer the dough to a lightly floured work surface and knead gently just until it comes together into a smooth, firm ball. Divide the dough into 4 equal pieces; each will weigh about 325 grams (11½ ounces). Brush each ball very lightly with oil and then put each ball into a loosely fitting resealable plastic bag. Seal the bags, leaving room for the dough to rise, and refrigerate for at least 24 hours or up to 72 hours for the best results.

- 800 grams bread flour
- 2 ½ teaspoons kosher salt
- 1 teaspoon instant dry yeast
- 2 teaspoons sugar
- 2 ¼ cups lukewarm water (80°F to 90°F)
- 2 tablespoons olive oil, plus more for brushing

This is also an excellent dough recipe, but it is quite different from the thin-crust dough recipe. Once again a scale and good flour are important. As with their thin-crust pizza dough, Ginny and Kim Youngblood clearly did their homework when they created this recipe, because this is the real thing for a proper deep-dish pizza.

Ginny and Kim's Deep-Dish Pizza Dough MAKES DOUGH FOR ONE 14-INCH DEEP-DISH PIZZA

400 grams bread flour

140 grams semolina flour

1½ cups lukewarm water
(80°F to 90°F)

1 teaspoon instant dry yeast

¼ teaspoon kosher salt

1 teaspoon olive oil

4 tablespoons salted butter,
melted and cooled

1½ teaspoons sugar

1 teaspoon cream of tartar

In a large bowl, combine the bread flour, semolina flour, yeast, and salt. Stir to mix well and then let rest for 5 to 10 minutes to allow the yeast to combine with the flour. Add the water a little at a time while mixing with a wooden spoon. Continue to mix with the spoon until all of the dry ingredients are evenly moistened and incorporated. Then, using your hands, shape the dough into a ball in the bowl. It will be wet and sticky. Cover the bowl with a towel and let the dough rest for 25 minutes in a warm part of the kitchen.

Lightly dust a work surface with bread flour and turn out the dough onto the floured surface. Add the oil, butter, sugar, and cream of tartar and knead for just 1 to 2 minutes, until the new ingredients are incorporated. Oil the inside of a large resealable plastic bag and place the dough in the bag. Seal the bag, leaving room for the dough to rise, and refrigerate for 24 hours before using.

For many pizza partisans, the sauce on a pizza is the most important taste, and this one will make those folks happy. It's simple and best made a day ahead of time and is far better than the stuff in a jar. The only change I would make is to add some red pepper flakes if you like it spicy.

Ginny and Kim's Pizza Sauce

MAKES ABOUT 3 CUPS, ENOUGH FOR FOUR 14-INCH THIN-CRUST PIZZAS OR ONE 14-INCH DEEP-DISH PIZZA

Combine all of the ingredients in a large glass bowl and whisk until well blended. Cover and let rest for 12 to 24 hours at room temperature. Before using, whisk again thoroughly. This sauce will keep in an airtight container in the refrigerator for up to 1 week.

1 (28-ounce) can good-quality Italian crushed tomatoes, with juices

1 tablespoon dried oregano leaves

1 tablespoon dried basil leaves

1 tablespoon granulated garlic

1 teaspoon sugar

½ teaspoon red pepper flakes (optional)

This is the kind of pizza everyone thinks Chicagoans eat, and although it has become more popular, most of the attention it gets comes from tourists. That being said, it is a very good thing to eat, and Ginny and Kim's dough really hits the mark. The crust should have a crusty, chewy, bread-like consistency, as this one does. The Big Green Egg ceramic deep-dish pizza stone is perfect for realizing that goal. I add a piece of parchment to be sure the crust won't stick, but Kim tells me that since his pan is now smooth and well seasoned, he no longer needs the parchment. I used pepperoni here, but feel free to add what you want. Just be sure to precook any sausage or vegetables and don't add too much topping or you will end up with a mudslide.

Deep-Dish Tourist Pizza MAKES ONE 14-INCH DEEP-DISH PIZZA; 8 SERVINGS

Ginny and Kim's Deep-Dish Pizza Dough (page 86), at room temperature for 2 to 4 hours

8 ounces provolone cheese, sliced

8 ounces mozzarella cheese, sliced

4 ounces pepperoni, sliced

3 cups Ginny and Kim's Pizza Sauce (page 87) or favorite pizza or marinara sauce

2 tablespoons honey

½ cup grated Parmesan cheese

Prepare the EGG to cook indirect at 400°F. Place a flat pizza stone on the EGG cooking grid and preheat it for 30 minutes.

Lightly dust a work surface with flour. Have ready a 14-inch deep-dish pizza stone or EGG-safe 14-inch deep-dish pizza pan. Using a rolling pin, roll out the dough for a 14-inch deep-dish pizza, using as little extra flour as possible, shaping it into a circle, and making sure it is large enough to cover the bottom and up the sides of the pizza pan. As the dough takes shape, transfer it to a 14-inch circle of parchment paper and continue to roll until it is the correct size. When the dough is ready, slide it on the parchment into the deep-dish pizza stone or pan, pushing it down into the corners and pulling the sides up to the top of the pan.

Top the dough with all of the provolone, overlapping the slices as needed. Add the mozzarella and again overlap the slices as necessary. Lay the pepperoni on top in a single layer. Gently pour the sauce over the pepperoni and then spread it evenly across the pizza. Drizzle the sauce with the honey. Sprinkle the Parmesan evenly over the top.

Place the pizza on top of the preheated flat pizza stone already in the EGG and cook for 20 minutes. Carefully spin the pizza 180 degrees to ensure even cooking and cook for another 20 to 30 minutes, until the crust is golden brown on the bottom and the middle of the pizza is bubbly hot.

Transfer the deep-dish pizza stone or pan to a heat-safe surface and let rest for 15 minutes. You can cut and serve the pizza from the pan or you can take the pizza out of the pan. To take it out, cut around the edge with a sharp knife to loosen it. Using a spatula and the parchment, slide the pizza out of the pan onto a cutting board or pizza pan. Remove and discard the parchment. Slice into 8 wedges and serve.

This is the kind of pizza that people who live in Chicago eat most of the time. Although deep-dish pizza is a very good thing, it isn't what is served in most of the pizzerias in the neighborhoods. Chicago pizza is typically made with the sausage placed on top of the cheese, and in the best places, it's arranged in a meticulous grid fashion so that each piece of pizza gets the perfect amount of sausage. It may have onions, peppers, or mushrooms added, depending on your taste. It's baked until the crust is crispy, and it's always cut into squares (the way God intended). Needless to say, I really like this kind of pizza, and the EGG makes a very good version. Peek underneath to get it cooked just how you like it. Well done for me, please.

Thin-Crust Real Chicago Pizza MAKES ONE 14-INCH PIZZA; ABOUT 4 SERVINGS

8 ounces Italian sausage

1 ball Ginny and Kim's Thin-Crust Pizza Dough (page 85), about 325 grams (11½ ounces), at room temperature for 2 to 4 hours

Bread flour, for dusting

½ cup Ginny and Kim's Pizza Sauce (page 87) or favorite pizza or marinara sauce

2 cups shredded mozzarella cheese

Prepare the EGG to cook indirect at 500°F. Place the pizza stone on the EGG cooking grid and preheat it for 30 minutes.

Divide the sausage into about 26 bite-size balls. They don't have to be perfect meatballs but should be a consistent size. Heat a large skillet over medium-high heat on the stove. Add the sausage balls and cook, stirring occasionally, for 5 to 7 minutes, until lightly browned and mostly cooked through. They will finish cooking as the pizza bakes. Transfer to a paper towel–lined bowl and set aside.

Lightly dust a work surface with flour. Using a rolling pin, roll out the dough for a 14-inch pizza, using as little extra flour as possible and shaping the dough into a circle. As the dough takes shape, transfer it to a 14-inch circle of parchment paper and continue to roll until it is the size of the parchment. When the dough is ready, slide the parchment with the pizza round onto a large pizza peel. Top with the sauce, spreading it all the way to the edges. Sprinkle the cheese over the sauce. Add the sausage in a grid pattern so that when you slice the pizza into squares, the sausage will be evenly distributed.

Slide the pizza on the parchment onto the hot pizza stone and cook for 8 minutes. Carefully spin the pizza 180 degrees to ensure even cooking and cook for another 7 to 8 minutes, until the crust is golden brown on the bottom and the top is bubbly hot. Slide the pizza back onto the pizza peel. Transfer the pizza to a pan or cutting board, removing the parchment if it's still there. Let rest for 5 minutes, then cut into squares to serve.

As a pizza purist, I must admit that this seemed a little strange to me until I tasted it. It's very creative and people think it's just amazing when you serve it. It's the ideal ending to a pizza party or just about any meal. I guess you could use other cookies or even dried fruits in place of the cookies, but I don't see why anyone would not want to use Oreos. Thanks Ginny and Kim Youngblood for all of your help with the pizzas here and especially for this one that is all you.

Ginny and Kim's Dessert Pizza MAKES ONE 14-INCH PIZZA; ABOUT 8 SERVINGS

1 cup confectioners' sugar, divided

1 teaspoon milk, or more if needed

1 ½ teaspoons vanilla extract, divided

1 ball Ginny and Kim's Thin-Crust Pizza Dough (page 85), about 325 grams (11 ½ ounces), at room temperature for 2 to 4 hours

8 ounces spreadable cream cheese, at room temperature

1 (14-ounce) package chocolate sandwich cookies

Prepare the EGG to cook indirect at 375°F. Place the pizza stone on the EGG cooking grid and preheat it for 30 minutes.

To make the topping, in a small bowl, combine ⅓ cup of the sugar, 1 teaspoon milk, and ½ teaspoon of the vanilla and mix well. This mixture should be just thin enough to drizzle onto the cooked pizza later. Add a little more milk if needed. Set aside.

Lightly dust a work surface with flour. Using a rolling pin, roll out the dough for a 14-inch pizza, using as little extra flour as possible and shaping the dough into a circle. As the dough takes shape, transfer it to a 14-inch circle of parchment paper and continue to roll until it is round, thin, and the size of the parchment. When the dough is ready, slide the parchment with the pizza round onto a large pizza peel.

In a medium bowl, combine the cream cheese and the remaining ⅔ cup sugar and 1 teaspoon vanilla and mix until blended and creamy. Spread the mixture evenly over the pizza dough. Place the cookies in a large resealable plastic bag and seal the bag, forcing out as much air as possible. Crush the cookies with a rolling pin, then sprinkle the crumbs evenly over the cream cheese mixture.

Slide the pizza on the parchment onto the hot stone and cook for 7 minutes. Spin the pizza 180 degrees to ensure even cooking and cook for another 6 to 8 minutes, until the crust is golden brown on the bottom and the cheese is hot and melted.

Slide the pizza back onto the pizza peel. You may lose the parchment in the transfer, but that's OK. Transfer the pizza to a pan or cutting board and immediately drizzle it with the reserved topping. Let rest for 5 minutes. Cut into 8 wedges to serve.

A calzone is simply a folded-over pizza. It starts out the same, you just put all the toppings on one half and fold the dough over before baking. Don't overfill it and make sure the fillings are cooked before you assemble it. Thanks to Rob at Big Green Egg for the tips on poking holes in the top and using the egg wash to help it brown. Seal it up real good and make a pretty edge if you can.

Fully Loaded Calzone MAKES 1 CALZONE; ABOUT 4 SERVINGS

1 tablespoon olive oil

4 ounces Italian sausage

½ medium green bell pepper, seeded and thinly sliced

½ medium red onion, thinly sliced

4 ounces baby bella (crimini) mushrooms, sliced

Kosher salt and ground pepper

¼ cup Ginny and Kim's Pizza Sauce (page 87) or favorite pizza or marinara sauce

1 ball Ginny and Kim's Thin-Crust Pizza Dough (page 85), about 325 grams (11½ ounces), at room temperature for 2 to 4 hours

½ cup shredded mozzarella cheese

1 large egg

1 tablespoon water

Prepare the EGG to cook indirect at 500°F. Place the pizza stone on the EGG cooking grid and preheat it for 30 minutes.

Heat the oil in a large skillet over medium-high heat on the stove. Crumble the sausage into the pan, breaking it into small pieces. Add the bell pepper, onion, and mushrooms, season with salt and pepper, and cook, stirring occasionally, for 10 to 12 minutes, until the sausage is cooked through and the onion and pepper are soft. Remove from the heat and stir in the sauce. Set aside to cool for at least 10 minutes.

Lightly dust a work surface with flour. Using a rolling pin, roll out the dough for a 14-inch pizza, using as little extra flour as possible and shaping the dough into a circle. As the dough takes shape, transfer it to a 14-inch circle of parchment paper and continue to roll until it is round, thin, and the size of the parchment. When the dough is ready, slide the parchment with the dough round onto a large pizza peel. Using tongs, place the sausage mixture on half of the dough, leaving behind as much liquid as possible. Top the sausage mixture with the cheese and fold the empty half of the dough over the filling. Starting at one corner of the half-moon, fold and crimp the seam a little at a time, sealing the edge as neatly as you can and continuing until the whole calzone is sealed. In a small bowl, whisk together the egg and water until blended.

Brush the calzone all over with the egg wash. Using a sharp knife, poke three 1-inch-long slits into the top of the calzone, spacing them about 1 inch apart.

Slide the calzone on the parchment onto the hot pizza stone and cook for 10 minutes. Carefully spin the calzone 180 degrees to ensure even cooking and cook for about 15 minutes longer, or until golden brown and crispy on the top and the bottom.

Slide the calzone back onto the pizza peel. You may lose the parchment in the transfer, but that's OK. Transfer the calzone to a plate or cutting board, removing the parchment if it's still there. Let rest for 5 minutes, then cut into 4 pieces to serve.

Garlic knots are that little something extra that the pizza man cooks up for the guests. They're simple to make and they're really tasty. The idea is to use the leftover dough, but I always keep a couple extra dough balls tucked away for making them. You can use fresh garlic if you like and cook them soft or crunchy, or you can top them with a sprinkle of grated Parmesan. There's no bad way to do it.

MAKES ABOUT 24 KNOTS # Homemade Garlic Knots

Prepare the EGG to cook indirect at 500°F. Place the pizza stone on the EGG cooking grid and preheat it for 30 minutes.

Lightly dust a work surface with flour. Roll out the dough into an 8 by 12-inch rectangle, using as little extra flour as possible. Place a 14-inch round piece of parchment on a large pizza peel. Using a pizza wheel or a butter knife, and starting at a short side, cut the dough into 1-inch-wide strips. Cut the strips into pieces about 4 inches long. You should have about 24 pieces. Tie each strip into a loose knot and lay it on the parchment, spacing the knots evenly.

Combine the granulated garlic, salt, parsley, pepper, and butter in a small bowl and mix well. Brush the knots all over with the butter mixture. Slide the parchment onto the hot pizza stone, close the EGG lid, and cook the knots for 15 to 20 minutes, until lightly browned on top and golden brown on the bottom.

Slide the parchment with the knots back onto the pizza peel and remove the knots from the EGG. Transfer to a platter and serve immediately.

1 ball Ginny and Kim's Thin-Crust Pizza Dough (page 85), about 325 grams (11 ½ ounces), at room temperature for 2 to 4 hours

½ teaspoon granulated garlic

½ teaspoon kosher salt

½ teaspoon dried parsley leaves

¼ teaspoon black pepper

4 tablespoons salted butter, melted and cooled

These cupcakes, which are kind of like tasty breadless meat loaf sandwiches, can be served warm or at room temperature and make great tailgate food. You can eat a cupcake with one hand and hold your drink in the other. I use jalapeño jelly from the supermarket for this recipe, but there are plenty of fiery exotic pepper jellies available, so use what you like and can find locally.

Pepper Jelly Meat Loaf Cupcakes MAKES 6 SERVINGS

1½ pounds ground beef (80 percent lean)

1 teaspoon kosher salt

½ teaspoon black pepper

¼ cup finely chopped yellow onion

1 large jalapeño chile, seeded and finely chopped

3 large eggs, lightly beaten

½ cup plus 2 tablespoons pepper jelly, divided

⅓ cup dried bread crumbs

¼ cup ketchup

Prepare the EGG to cook indirect at 375°F. Using your hands, break up the beef so it is loose, capturing it in a large bowl. Sprinkle the meat with the salt, pepper, onion, and chile, distributing them evenly. Pour the eggs over the top and add 2 tablespoons of the pepper jelly. Using your hands, mix until all of the ingredients are evenly incorporated. Sprinkle the bread crumbs over the mixture and again mix with your hands until fully blended.

Spray a 6-cup standard muffin pan (about 3-inch cups) with vegetable cooking spray. Divide the meat mixture into 6 equal portions and shape each portion into a ball. Shape 1 ball so it will fit snugly in a muffin cup, place it in a prepared cup, and press gently to flatten the top. Repeat with the remaining 5 balls. Place the pan in the EGG on the cooking grid and cook for 20 minutes, or until the cupcakes are firm enough to remove from the pan.

Remove the muffin pan from the EGG and invert the pan to dump the cupcakes out onto a work surface. Return the cupcakes, right side up, to the EGG grid and continue cooking for 5 minutes more.

In a small bowl, whisk together the ketchup and the remaining ½ cup jelly. Spoon the jelly mixture over the cupcakes and cook for 15 to 20 minutes, until the glaze is well set and the cupcakes have reached an internal temperature of 160°F.

Transfer the cupcakes to a platter and let rest for at least 5 minutes before serving. Serve warm or at room temperature.

Chicken bog is a South Carolina thing, and as far as I can tell, it's one of those beloved local dishes like jambalaya, Brunswick stew, and burgoo. These are typically designed to feed a lot of people good food on a small budget and are often served at church and community gatherings. They utilize rice or other inexpensive tasty things and are made in big batches, and although they are not typically baked, the technique works well in the EGG. This is a simple recipe of chicken and rice and not much else. You'll be tempted to add things and feel free to do that, but if you want the original, resist that urge and make this tasty dish just as I have.

MAKES 6 SERVINGS Southern Chicken Bog

Prepare the EGG to cook indirect at 375°F with apple wood added for smoke flavor. Place a cast-iron Dutch oven on the cooking grid and preheat it for 10 minutes.

Add the oil to the Dutch oven and stir it to cover the bottom. Add the onion, garlic, celery, chicken, sausage, salt, and pepper and mix well. Cook, stirring once at about the halfway point, for 30 minutes, or until the chicken is cooked.

Add the 2 cups broth, water, and bay leaf and mix well. Cook for 30 minutes. Add the rice and mix well. Cook for 15 minutes. Stir well and add a little more broth if the mixture looks dry at this point. Continue to cook for 15 minutes, or until the rice is tender. There should be just a little liquid in the bottom of the Dutch oven. If there isn't any, add a little broth, and if there is a lot, cook for another 5 minutes.

Remove from the EGG and sprinkle with the parsley before serving.

¼ cup olive oil

1 small yellow onion, finely chopped

1 clove garlic, crushed

1 stalk celery, finely chopped

1 pound boneless, skinless chicken thighs, cut into large dice

8 ounces smoked sausage, cut into medium dice

1 teaspoon kosher salt

1 teaspoon black pepper

2 cups chicken broth, plus more if needed

2 cups water

1 bay leaf

1 cup long-grain white rice

2 tablespoons chopped fresh curly parsley

Everybody loves mac and cheese and everybody loves burgers, so this dish should be a double-whammy favorite. I just cook some extra burgers earlier in the week and then I have the leftovers to make this. If not, just cook the burgers first. That extra flavor from grilling them first is key. The assembly is a little different when you do a casserole completely on the EGG, but it works well, and there's not much cleanup in the kitchen when you get done. For a little extra zip, add a couple of minced jalapeños, or switch up the cheese for a Swiss burger if you like. Anything that goes well on a cheeseburger will go well in this casserole.

Mac and Cheeseburger Casserole MAKES 4 TO 6 SERVINGS

¼ cup olive oil

1 small yellow onion, halved lengthwise and thinly sliced

1 pound cooked hamburgers, crumbled

¼ cup all-purpose flour

2 cups milk

½ teaspoon kosher salt

½ teaspoon black pepper

2 cups grated mild cheddar cheese

2 cups cooked elbow macaroni

4 medium Roma tomatoes, seeded and cut into small dice

4 slices thick-cut bacon, cooked and finely chopped

½ cup panko (Japanese bread crumbs)

Prepare the EGG to cook indirect at 375°F. Place a cast-iron Dutch oven on the cooking grid and preheat it for 10 minutes.

Add the oil and onion to the Dutch oven and stir to coat the onion with the oil. Add the burgers and mix well. Cook, stirring occasionally, for about 10 minutes, or until the onion begins to soften. Add the flour and mix well. Cook for 5 minutes. Add the milk and mix well. Cook, stirring occasionally, for about 10 minutes, or until the milk begins to simmer. Add the salt, pepper, and cheese and mix well. Cook for 2 to 3 minutes to melt the cheese. Mix again, stir in the macaroni, and then gently fold in the tomatoes.

In a small bowl, mix together the bacon and bread crumbs. Sprinkle it evenly over the casserole. Cook for about 30 minutes, or until the top is golden brown and the casserole is bubbling hot. Remove from the EGG and serve immediately.

This dish was a staple of my childhood. My mom would bake a ham just so she would have leftovers to make it. No cheese is added in the Lampe family version, just a tasty white sauce with ham. My sister, Denise, still considers it one of her best dishes, and I'm happy when she makes it. It's important to slice the potatoes thinly. I use a mandoline, but with patience and a sharp knife, you can get it done without one. This is a great dish to cook in a disposable aluminum foil pan to avoid a messy cleanup.

Scalloped Potatoes with Ham

MAKES ABOUT 8 SERVINGS

Prepare the EGG to cook indirect at 375°F. Melt the butter in a medium saucepan over medium heat on the stove. Add the flour, stir to rid the mixture of any lumps, and then cook, stirring often, for about 1 minute to cook the flour. Gradually add the half-and-half while whisking constantly until blended. Add the salt, pepper, granulated garlic and onion, and nutmeg and whisk until blended. Continue cooking, stirring often, until the sauce comes to a simmer and begins to thicken. Remove from the heat.

Peel the potatoes and then slice them thinly using a mandoline or a sharp chef's knife. Spray a 9 by 13-inch EGG-safe baking pan with vegetable cooking spray. Layer one-third of the potato slices in the bottom of the prepared baking pan, overlapping them as needed. Top with the ham, distributing it evenly across the potatoes. Sprinkle half of the parsley evenly over the ham. Spoon one-third of the sauce evenly over the potatoes. Top with the remaining potatoes and then the remaining parsley. Spoon the remaining sauce evenly over the potatoes, making sure all of the potatoes are covered. Sprinkle lightly with paprika to help with browning.

Place the pan in the EGG and cook for 30 minutes. Spin the pan 180 degrees to ensure even cooking and cook for another 30 minutes. The potatoes should be golden brown and bubbly hot. Check for tenderness with a skewer or knife, and if they are very tender, they are done. If not, cook for another 15 minutes, or until they are tender.

Remove the pan from the EGG and let the casserole rest for 5 minutes before serving.

4 tablespoons salted butter

¼ cup all-purpose flour

3 cups half-and-half

2 teaspoons kosher salt

1 teaspoon black pepper

1 teaspoon granulated garlic

1 teaspoon granulated onion

¼ teaspoon ground nutmeg

3 pounds russet potatoes

2 cups diced ham

2 tablespoons minced fresh curly parsley

Paprika

I once watched baking legend Nick Malgieri make a divine zucchini tart with an olive oil crust, and I knew that someday I would make a version that worked on the EGG. Well, here it is. Salting and draining the zucchini is straight from that class with Nick, and it's really important. Once that is done, the zucchini has a lot less liquid in it and can be incorporated into a filling without a problem. I grate the zucchini with my food processor and find that the texture is perfect that way. This pie solves that problem of too many zucchini when these high-yield squashes are in season. My sister in Wisconsin says she has to lock her car during the harvest season or someone will put a bag of them in it.

Summertime Zucchini Pie MAKES 8 SERVINGS

3 medium zucchini

1½ teaspoons kosher salt

1 rolled pie crust for a 9-inch pie

2 large eggs

½ cup milk

½ cup finely chopped red onion

Finely grated zest of 1 navel orange

½ teaspoon black pepper

½ teaspoon ground nutmeg

A couple hours before you plan to cook, grate the zucchini in a food processor fitted with the grating blade. You should have 4 cups. Put the zucchini in a large bowl and sprinkle with the salt. Toss to mix. Place the zucchini in a large, fine-mesh sieve over a bowl or the sink so the zucchini can drain. Let drain for 2 hours, tossing it twice during that time.

Prepare the EGG to cook indirect at 375°F with clean lump charcoal. Line an EGG-safe 9-inch fluted tart pan with removable bottom with the pie crust, lightly pressing it into the corners and up the sides of the pan and trimming away any excess along the rim. With the tip of a knife, poke 20 evenly spaced holes in the bottom of the crust. Line the crust with parchment paper and top with pie weights, dried beans, or uncooked rice to hold it down. Put the tart pan on the EGG cooking grid and blind bake the crust for 15 minutes.

Meanwhile, to make the filling, in a large bowl, whisk together the eggs and milk until blended. Add the onion, orange zest, pepper, and nutmeg and mix well. Add the zucchini and toss until fully mixed.

When the crust is ready, transfer the pan to a work surface and remove the weights and paper. Pour the filling into the crust and spread evenly all the way to the edges. Put the pie in the EGG and cook for 20 minutes. Spin the pie 180 degrees to ensure even cooking and continue cooking for about 20 minutes, or until the pie is firm to the touch and golden brown.

Remove the pie from the EGG, let rest for 5 minutes, then slip off the outer ring. Slide the tart onto a plate and serve warm or at room temperature.

These may be simple, but they sure are tasty and in everyone's comfort food zone. They're kind of a poor man's pizza for when you don't want to make the dough. Serve them whole as a snack or serve a couple of them as a light lunch. You can quarter them, too, and offer them as an appetizer. Feel free to substitute your favorite cheese or trade the ham out for prosciutto, salami, or pepperoni. Just don't overload them or you'll need a clean shirt.

Ham and Cheese Toasty MAKES 8 SERVINGS

⅓ cup mayonnaise

½ teaspoon dry mustard

½ teaspoon chili powder

4 English muffins, split

1 cup finely diced ham

2 cups shredded sharp cheddar
  cheese

Prepare the EGG to cook indirect at 450°F with the pizza stone on the cooking grid.

In a small bowl, combine the mayonnaise, mustard, and chili powder and mix well. Spread a thin layer of the mayonnaise mixture on the cut side of the English muffins, using it all. Divide the ham evenly among the muffin halves, spreading it evenly to the edge. Top each muffin half with an equal portion of the cheese, using it all.

Place the muffins on the hot pizza stone and cook for 12 to 15 minutes, until they are crispy and bubbly hot. Transfer to a platter and serve hot or at room temperature.

The most decadent of all dinners is a perfectly cooked lobster tail. Lobster tails are best when baked on top of the shell, both for taste and presentation, and because these have a little EGG flavor, they are the tastiest you will ever have. Lobster tails are typically sold frozen, so buy them a couple of days ahead and defrost in the refrigerator. Cutting them out of the shell is a little tricky, but with a good pair of kitchen shears and a little patience, you should be able to do it.

MAKES 4 SERVINGS Baked Lobster Tails

Prepare the EGG to cook indirect at 350°F. With a good pair of kitchen shears and starting at the big end, cut the top shell of a lobster tail right down the center all the way to the tail fins. With your hands, open the cut shell wide enough to pull the meat out, leaving just the tip of the tail attached and trying not to break the shell in half. Hold the meat away from the shell and close the shell back up under the meat. Lay the meat back on top. If the meat detaches it will still work. Use the shears to trim away any loose or small pieces on the sides of the meat. These will overcook and become tough when you cook the tail. Repeat with the remaining tails. Place all of the tails on a large perforated grid.

Place 4 tablespoons of the butter in a small microwave-safe bowl and microwave on high for about 45 seconds, or until melted. Add the granulated garlic and paprika and mix well. Brush the lobster tails with the butter mixture, place them on the cooking grid in the EGG, and cook for about 25 minutes, or until the tails are opaque, slightly firm, and have reached an internal temperature of 140°F in the thickest part.

Place the remaining ½ cup butter in a medium microwave-safe bowl and microwave on high for about 45 seconds, or until melted. Divide the butter evenly among 4 small bowls. Serve each guest a tail with a portion of butter and a couple of the lemon wedges.

4 (12-ounce) lobster tails

4 tablespoons plus ½ cup salted butter, divided

½ teaspoon granulated garlic

½ teaspoon paprika

1 lemon, cut into 8 wedges

I've always enjoyed making and eating double-baked potatoes. There are so many variations that work well, and they go with just about anything. If you add just enough cream or milk to get the consistency correct and then taste to make sure the seasoning is right before you reload them, you can't go wrong. This combination of green onions, ham, and Swiss cheese is my current favorite, but I like bacon, cheddar, and a little chili powder, too. If serving these potatoes family-style or on a buffet table, cut some of them in half for the lighter eaters and leave the remainder whole for the heartier eaters.

Swiss Cheesy Double-Baked Potatoes MAKES 6 SERVINGS

3 large russet potatoes

1 tablespoon olive oil

2 teaspoons kosher salt, divided

1 teaspoon black pepper

½ cup half-and-half

8 green onions, white and firm green parts, thinly sliced

1 cup finely chopped ham

2 cups shredded Swiss cheese

Paprika, for sprinkling

Prepare the EGG to cook indirect at 375°F. Scrub and dry the potatoes. Brush them all over with the oil, then season them all over with 1 teaspoon of the salt. Place the potatoes directly on the EGG cooking grid and cook until soft, about 1¼ hours. Transfer the potatoes to a plate to cool for at least 30 minutes or up to 1 hour.

Cut each potato in half lengthwise to create 2 nice boats. Using a spoon, scoop out all of the flesh from each potato boat, being careful not to tear the skin. Put all of the potato flesh in a large microwave-safe bowl. Set the skins aside. Microwave the potato flesh on high for 1 to 2 minutes, until warm. Add the remaining 1 teaspoon salt, the pepper, and the half-and-half and mash the potatoes with a potato masher until smooth. Add the green onions, ham, and cheese and mix with a spoon until well blended. If the cheese is not mixing in well, heat the whole mixture for another minute in the microwave. When everything is well blended, scoop the potato mixture into the reserved skins, distributing it evenly and mounding it high. Smooth out the tops with the back of a spoon and then sprinkle them lightly with paprika.

Return the potatoes to the EGG grid and cook for 30 minutes, or until heated through and lightly browned. Serve hot.

Stuffmuffins are a new Dr. BBQ invention, and I really think these are going to catch on. They make nice individual servings with gravy—like traditional stuffing—at the dinner table, but they also travel well for tailgating. They're tasty warm or at room temperature, and best of all, everybody gets a good portion of the coveted crunchy edges. This version has a bit of New Orleans flair, but you can substitute any cooked sausage and change up the spices any way you like.

MAKES 12 SERVINGS # Stuffmuffins

Prepare the EGG to cook indirect at 375°F. Melt the butter in a large saucepan over medium heat on the stove. Add the sausage, onion, celery, chiles, pepper, and salt, mix well, and cook, stirring occasionally, for 6 to 7 minutes, until the onion and celery are soft. Remove from the heat and add the broth. Place the stuffing mix in a large bowl. Pour the vegetable mixture over the top and mix with a spoon until evenly moistened and well blended.

Spray a 12-cup standard muffin pan (about 3-inch cups) with vegetable cooking spray. Spoon the stuffing into the muffin cups, dividing it equally. Smooth and shape the top of each "muffin" without packing the muffin too tightly. Place the muffin pan in the EGG and cook for 15 minutes. Rotate the muffin pan 180 degrees to ensure even cooking and continue to cook for 10 to 15 minutes, until the edges of the muffins are golden brown and the tops are slightly crispy.

Remove the muffin pan from the EGG and let the muffins cool in the pan for 5 minutes. Gently remove each muffin from the pan and serve warm or at room temperature.

½ cup salted butter

1 cup finely diced andouille sausage

1 cup finely chopped yellow onion

1 cup finely chopped celery

2 jalapeño chiles, seeded and finely chopped

1 teaspoon black pepper

½ teaspoon kosher salt

2 cups vegetable broth

1 (14-ounce) package corn bread stuffing

Baking cookies on the EGG is one of those things that will amaze your friends and make them jealous of your EGG. I like to keep the dough cold until the cookies are ready to go, so they don't spread too much while they bake. I also like to cook them on parchment paper so they are easy to handle when they're hot. If you don't have a big pizza pan, you can use any sheet pan, though you will need to divide the dough into three batches if the baking surface is smaller. Feel free to substitute any type of chocolate or dried fruit in this recipe. You can also just use your favorite cookie recipe. It will work fine on the EGG.

White Chocolate Chip–Cherry Cookies

MAKES 20 COOKIES

In the bowl of a stand mixer fitted with the paddle attachment, combine the butter, both sugars, vanilla, salt, and baking soda.
With the mixer on low speed mix everything for 1 minute. Increase the mixer speed to medium and mix, stopping occasionally to scrape down the sides of the bowl, for about 4 minutes, or until the batter is fluffy and pale in color. Add the egg and continue mixing for about 2 minutes, or until the batter is smooth. Add the flour in three batches, mixing until incorporated after each addition and stopping to scrape down the bowl as needed. When the final flour is added, continue mixing just until a dough forms. Remove the paddle and take the bowl off of the mixer stand. Add the white chocolate chips and the cherries and fold them in by hand until evenly distributed. Transfer the dough to a clean bowl. Cover and refrigerate for 1 hour.

Prepare the EGG to cook indirect at 350°F. Line a large pizza pan with parchment paper. Divide the dough in half and return one half to the refrigerator. Divide the other half into 10 balls of about 2 tablespoons each. Place the balls on the prepared pizza pan, spacing them about 2 inches apart. Place the pan in the EGG and cook for 6 minutes. Rotate the pan 180 degrees to ensure even cooking and continue to cook for 5 to 7 minutes, or until the cookies are golden brown on the bottom and have puffed up.

Remove the pan from the EGG and quickly slide the parchment with the cookies onto a counter to cool. This will keep them from overcooking. Add a new piece of parchment and repeat with the remaining dough. Let the cookies cool for 15 minutes before eating, if you can resist.

- ½ cup salted butter, at room temperature
- ⅓ cup granulated sugar
- ½ cup firmly packed light brown sugar
- 2 teaspoons vanilla extract
- ½ teaspoon kosher salt
- ½ teaspoon baking soda
- 1 large egg
- 1 ½ cups all-purpose flour
- ⅔ cup white chocolate chips
- ½ cup dried cherries

I've made this cake at many EGGfests and Big Green Egg events over the years. Only your EGGhead friends will get it. You'll need to add the whole little bottle of food coloring for the color to be right. It doesn't really need the peppermint flavor, since the cake mix is good out of the box. Or you could make it a different flavor, like lemon, almond, or orange. But when you see how green the cake is, I think you'll agree that peppermint is the right flavor for it.

Green Velvet Cake MAKES 8 SERVINGS

1 box extra-moist white cake mix

Water, vegetable oil, and eggs, according to directions on cake mix box

1 (1-ounce) bottle liquid green food coloring

1 teaspoon peppermint extract

FROSTING

½ cup salted butter, at room temperature

8 ounces cream cheese, at room temperature

1 teaspoon vanilla extract

1 pound confectioners' sugar (about 4 cups)

Green sprinkles, for decorating

Prepare the EGG to cook indirect at 375°F. Spray a 10-inch (12-cup) Bundt pan with vegetable cooking spray. Prepare the cake mix as directed on the box, using the water, vegetable oil, and eggs. Add the food coloring and peppermint extract to the batter and mix well. Pour the batter into the prepared pan, spreading it evenly.

Place the pan in the EGG and cook for 15 minutes. Rotate the pan a one-third turn and cook for another 15 minutes. Rotate the pan another one-third turn and cook, checking often by inserting a toothpick deep into the center, for 10 to 20 minutes, until the toothpick comes out clean.

Transfer the pan to a sheet pan and let the cake cool for 20 minutes. Turn the cake out of the pan onto a large plate and let cool for 30 minutes longer, or until fully cooled.

Meanwhile, make the frosting. Combine the butter and cream cheese in a large bowl and beat with an electric mixer on medium speed until well blended. Add the vanilla and mix just until combined. On medium speed, add the sugar, 1 cup at a time, mixing until fully incorporated after each addition. The frosting should be smooth and creamy once the final addition is incorporated.

Using an icing spatula, frost the cake all over, applying the frosting in an even layer. Sprinkle the green sprinkles evenly over the frosted cake.

This recipe comes from my good friend Marsha Manley Hale, who lives in Lynchburg, Tennessee, and works at the Jack Daniel Distillery. If you've never been there, you really should plan a visit. It's the real thing and a lot of fun. Marsha is also a great southern cook and has a Big Green Egg right outside of her kitchen. I always include a recipe from her in my books. It's partly personal, because I like having her recipes for myself and I hope you do too. In this recipe, Marsha has combined the classic pecan pie with salted caramel and the great taste of Jack Daniel's Tennessee Honey whiskey.

Tennessee Honey-Caramel
MAKES 8 SERVINGS Pecan Pie

Prepare the EGG to cook indirect at 350°F. In a large bowl, combine the granulated sugar, corn syrup, salt, flour, and eggs and mix with an electric mixer on medium speed for about 3 minutes, or until combined. Add the vanilla, whiskey, butter, and pecans and, using a wooden spoon, mix until fully blended. Pour into the unbaked pie shell.

Place the pie in the EGG and cook for about 1¼ hours, or until the center appears set and a toothpick inserted into it comes out clean. Remove the pie from the EGG and place it on a wire rack to cool. Drizzle the caramel sauce evenly over the warm pie. Let rest at room temperature for 2 hours to set.

Just before serving, make the whipped cream. In a chilled bowl, beat the cream with the electric mixer on high speed until it just begins to form soft peaks. Add the confectioners' sugar and whiskey and continue to beat until stiff peaks form.

Slice the pie into 8 wedges. Top each serving with a dollop of the whipped cream.

¾ cup granulated sugar

1½ cups dark corn syrup

½ teaspoon kosher salt

1½ teaspoons all-purpose flour

3 large eggs

1 teaspoon vanilla extract

3 tablespoons Jack Daniel's Tennessee Honey Whiskey

1½ tablespoons salted butter, melted

1¾ cups pecan halves

¼ cup salted caramel sauce

1 (9-inch) unbaked pie shell

WHIPPED CREAM

1 cup heavy cream

¼ cup confectioners' sugar

1 tablespoon Jack Daniel's Tennessee Honey whiskey

This recipe multiplies easily. Make a lot because your guests are going to love them. I know this isn't a totally new recipe. It's probably lifted from the Girl Scouts or someone like that. But these aren't the same old burnt marshmallow s'mores. In my version, you wrap them all up ahead of time and then they're all ready at the same time and served in nice little packages. I started making these at trade shows because I needed to feed a lot of EGGcited people at the same time.

Wrapped S'mores MAKES 12 SERVINGS

24 square graham crackers

12 large pieces chocolate candy bar

12 large marshmallows

Prepare the EGG to cook indirect at 325°F. Cut 12 (12-inch) squares of aluminum foil. Lay a graham cracker square in the center of each foil square, top it with a piece of chocolate, followed by a marshmallow, and then another graham cracker square. Fold the foil up loosely on all sides, using it to keep everything in a nice, tidy stack. Close the top loosely and keep the packets in the upright position at all times.

Place the packets in the EGG and cook for about 15 minutes, or until the chocolate and marshmallow are melted. It's OK to peek to check. Transfer them to a platter and serve.

These are a simple and easy dessert that bakes well on the EGG. Everyone loves the taste of warm caramel and apples. Adding a scoop of vanilla ice cream when serving is a great finish. I like to have these ready to go at the end of a meal and put them in when the entrée comes off the EGG. By the time dinner is served and the table is cleaned up, a hot, fresh dessert is ready to be enjoyed.

MAKES 6 SERVINGS # Caramel Baked Apples

Prepare the EGG to cook indirect at 350°F. Using a melon baller, hollow out the apples to create a round hole on top about 1¼ inches across, being careful not to puncture the bottom. Place the apples in a pan. Pour the caramel topping into the apples, filling them about three quarters full. Top each with 5 mini marshmallows, squeezing them together to fit and pushing them down into the hole.

Cook for about 1 hour, until the apples are soft. Place each apple on a serving plate and drizzle with a little more of the caramel topping.

6 big round apples, like Jonagold or Fuji

1 cup caramel ice cream topping

30 mini marshmallows

Chapter 6

Roasting

Roasting on the EGG looks a lot like baking and frankly the process is very similar. The term *roasting* refers to cooking something that has structure to it, like meats and vegetables. Baking is reserved for things that will develop their structure during the cooking process, such as breads, cakes, and cookies. In the real world of cooking you can call it whatever you like as long as you do it right. Roasting is what your grandma did to that beef roast or the Thanksgiving turkey that made the meat perfectly cooked inside and beautifully browned on the outside. Roasting is also what modern chefs do to brussels sprouts and beets and butternut squash to soften the flesh and to develop great flavor via those browned bits on the outside. Most folks are limited to roasting in their oven, where the heat offers no additional flavor beyond the caramelization.

EGGheads are lucky to be able to roast in their EGGs, which adds a whole other layer of flavor from the charcoal. Think of that taste from a wood-fired pizza oven in a restaurant. It's not really smoky, but there is definitely a little pop of flavor from the wood that makes the food extra tasty. In the case of EGG cooking, it's the lump charcoal, which is essentially charred hickory and oak wood. I rarely add additional wood for flavor when I'm roasting. I like that mild hint of wood flavor from the lump charcoal, and for my taste, it's enough. I'm all for smoking food like I do in chapter 4, but then I'll season, sauce, and cook differently to match the recipe.

You'll find that the roasted meats and roasted vegetables in this chapter pair well with each other. If you're lucky enough to have two EGGs, this will be a good day to fire them both up. But if you don't have a pair, just nestle the side dish in alongside the main course, or use a double-decker setup and they'll get along well. A little bit of dripping on each other won't hurt a thing, either, as long as the food gets cooked through.

Most of the recipes in this chapter are roasted in the 350°F to 400°F range, which creates the wonderful side effects of caramelizing and browning. There are some notable exceptions, however. I go a little lower for bigger cuts and a little higher for anything that I want extra crispy. The recipes are mostly meaty roasts and large vegetable dishes meant for a family-style dinner, but I've snuck in a few surprises that will fit right in as an appetizer or small plate.

I love roasted garlic in my everyday cooking because it offers that great garlic flavor in a mellower and sweeter incarnation. Plus it keeps vampires away. But in this soup, the roasted garlic is the featured flavor and it's a good one. My fiancée, Sandi, really likes this soup, so I can serve it on date night. It's fine as long as you both eat it. Garnish with toasty croutons, chopped chives, and/or cooked chopped bacon, a favorite at my house.

EGG Roasted Garlic Soup MAKES ABOUT 6 SERVINGS

4 large heads garlic

2 tablespoons olive oil, plus more for brushing

Kosher salt and black pepper

½ medium white onion, finely chopped

6 tablespoons salted butter

½ cup all-purpose flour

4 cups vegetable broth, divided

1 cup water

Leaves of 3 small thyme sprigs

1 teaspoon kosher salt

½ teaspoon black pepper

1 cup heavy cream

Croutons, for serving

Chopped fresh curly parsley, for serving

Chopped cooked bacon, for serving

Prepare the EGG to cook indirect at 375°F. With a sharp knife, cut the pointy tops off of the heads of garlic to reveal the tips of the cloves. Place the heads on a small perforated grid or in an EGG proof dish. Brush the heads all over with oil and season with salt and pepper.

Place the garlic in the EGG and cook for about 45 minutes, or until the garlic is soft and golden brown on top.

Remove the garlic from the EGG and let cool completely. Squeeze the cooled cloves from their skin, being careful to keep the soft garlic and skins separate. Discard the skins.

Heat the 2 tablespoons oil in a large saucepan over medium heat on the stove. Add the onion and cook, stirring occasionally, for about 4 minutes, or until the onion is soft. Add the butter and cook until it has melted. Add the flour and garlic and cook, stirring often and smashing the garlic, for about 5 minutes, or until golden brown. Add 2 cups of the broth and cook, stirring often, until smooth. Add the remaining 2 cups broth along with the water, thyme, salt, and pepper. Mix well and bring just to a simmer. Remove from the heat and let cool slightly.

Pour half of the soup into a blender and blend on high speed for 1 minute, or until smooth. Transfer the puréed soup to a different large saucepan. Pour the remaining half into the blender and blend on high for 1 minute, or until smooth. Pour the second batch of puréed soup into the saucepan holding the first batch and place over medium heat. Bring to a simmer and then lower the heat to maintain a gentle simmer. Cook, stirring often, for about 5 minutes, or until thickened. Add the cream, mix well, and continue to cook, stirring often, until the soup returns to a simmer.

Remove from the heat, ladle into bowls, and garnish with the croutons, parsley, and bacon.

A real *porchetta* roast is pork belly with the skin on and wrapped around a highly seasoned boneless loin—an Italian delicacy for sure. This is not a simple item to find or cook properly for the home cook, so I've decided to simplify it with a common cut of pork and all of the same great seasonings as the original. It's best when assembled a day early so all of the flavors have time to blend. If you're not comfortable butterflying the roast, ask the butcher to do it at the store.

Porchetta-Style Pork Roast MAKES ABOUT 6 SERVINGS

1 teaspoon fennel seeds

4 teaspoons kosher salt

1 tablespoon coarsely chopped fresh rosemary

6 large fresh sage leaves, chopped

½ teaspoon red pepper flakes

½ teaspoon black pepper

Finely grated zest of 1 orange

6 cloves garlic, crushed

¼ cup olive oil

1 (4-pound) boneless pork shoulder roast

A day before you plan to cook, add the fennel seeds to a medium bowl. With a metal spoon, crush the seeds just to break them up. Add the salt and crush again to break up the seeds a little more. Add the rosemary, sage, pepper flakes, black pepper, orange zest, and garlic. Smash and mix with a spoon to break down the herbs. Add the oil and mix well. Set aside.

Take any string or netting off of the roast. Using a sharp knife with the blade held parallel to your cutting surface, butterfly the roast, cutting along the length of the pork shoulder but not all the way through, unfolding it as you go so you can open the meat like a book into a large flat slab. Cut a deep slash in any thick parts. Smear the fennel paste all over the top surface of the meat. Roll the roast back up, jelly-roll style, tucking in any loose parts. Using kitchen string, retie the roast in multiple directions to hold everything together. Rub any extra oil and paste on the outside of the roast. Wrap the roast tightly in plastic wrap. Refrigerate for 24 hours.

At least 30 minutes or up to 1 hour before you plan to cook, take the roast out of the refrigerator. Prepare the EGG to cook indirect with a drip pan at 325°F. Place the roast, fat side up, in the EGG and cook for 3½ to 4 hours, until it reaches an internal temperature of 180°F deep in the center.

Transfer the roast to a platter, tent loosely with aluminum foil, and let rest for 10 minutes. Remove the string and slice against the grain about ½ inch thick. Depending on your roast and the butterfly job, the slices may not stay together. If this happens, just cut the meat into attractive pieces and serve it in a rustic fashion.

Everybody loves gyros, and these little meatballs are a fun and easy way to get that great taste cooking on your EGG. I like them small with traditional *tzatziki* sauce for dipping and served as an appetizer, but they'd also go well with a spicy red sauce and some rice or pasta for a main course. My *tzatziki* skips the dill, a personal preference, but feel free to add some dill or even some fresh mint to make it your own.

Gyro Meatballs with Tzatziki

MAKES ABOUT 20 SMALL MEATBALLS

Prepare the EGG to cook indirect at 375°F. To make the sauce, combine the yogurt and cucumber in a large bowl and mix well. Add the garlic, lemon juice, salt, and pepper and mix well. Check for salt and pepper and add more if needed. Transfer to a serving bowl and drizzle with the oil. Set aside at room temperature.

To make the meatballs, using your hands, break up the lamb into small pieces, capturing them in a large bowl. Add the egg, garlic, salt, pepper, oregano, granulated onion, and cumin and mix with your hands until well blended. Add the bread crumbs and mix well. Spray a round perforated grid with vegetable cooking spray. Form the meat mixture into 20 meatballs, each weighing about 1 ounce, and place them on the prepared grid.

Place the perforated grid in the EGG and cook for 10 minutes. Rotate the grid 180 degrees and cook for 10 minutes longer, or until the internal temperature of the meatballs reaches 160°F in the center. While the meatballs are cooking, place 1 grape tomato on each of 20 short bamboo skewers.

When the meatballs are ready, add a meatball to each of the skewers. Stand the skewers upright to serve. Accompany with the sauce for dipping.

SAUCE

2 cups plain Greek yogurt

1 English cucumber, shredded

3 cloves garlic, crushed

Juice of 1 lemon

1 tablespoon kosher salt

¼ teaspoon black pepper

1 tablespoon olive oil

MEATBALLS

1 pound ground lamb

1 large egg, lightly beaten

3 cloves garlic, crushed

2 teaspoons kosher salt

½ teaspoon black pepper

½ teaspoon dried oregano leaves

¼ teaspoon granulated onion

¼ teaspoon ground cumin

¼ cup dried bread crumbs

20 grape tomatoes

Prime rib is a bit of a misnomer because it doesn't have to be USDA prime meat to make it a good one. Most of us use a USDA choice-graded standing rib roast and call it prime rib. It's a favorite around Christmas because it's over-the-top decadent at the table. It looks great and serves up beautifully, and just about everyone loves it. This recipe uses a bone-in roast. I like it with the bones cut away and then tied back on for easy carving, but there's no reason not to cook it boneless if you prefer. In that case you'll want to buy a rib eye roast. An overcooked prime rib can be a big disappointment, so pay strict attention to the internal temperature. Serve it au jus with creamy horseradish.

Herbed-Up Prime Rib MAKES 4 TO 6 SERVINGS

1 (4-pound) bone-in standing rib roast

Kosher salt and black pepper

4 tablespoons salted butter, at room temperature

1 tablespoon finely chopped fresh basil

1 tablespoon finely chopped fresh tarragon

1 tablespoon finely chopped fresh rosemary

One hour before you plan to cook, take the roast out of the refrigerator. Prepare the EGG to cook indirect with a drip pan at 350°F. Season the roast on all sides with salt and pepper. In a small bowl, combine the butter, basil, tarragon, and rosemary and mix well. Spread the herb butter all over the roast, applying the heaviest layer to the fat cap.

Place the roast, fat side up, on the EGG cooking grid and cook for about 2 hours, or until it reaches an internal temperature deep in the center of 125°F for medium-rare.

Transfer the roast to a platter, tent loosely with foil, and let rest for at least 20 minutes or up to 30 minutes. Cut the meat away from the bones and slice the roast thickly or thinly against the grain as desired. Separate the leftover beef rib bones and serve them along with the meat.

A pork picnic is the front arm of the hog, and for some reason, it is usually sold in American supermarkets with the skin left on. They're sometimes sold cured like a ham, but for this recipe, buy a fresh one. If you want to have more browned bark on the outside, you can remove the skin, but I like to cook with it on. It makes for a juicy, tender roast. The picnic is what I call knuckle meat, and it has a silky mouthfeel that is different from a loin roast or ham.

Roasted Pork Picnic MAKES ABOUT 10 SERVINGS

1 (8 to 9-pound) skin-on whole
    fresh pork picnic

PASTE
4 large cloves garlic, crushed
1 tablespoon olive oil
1 teaspoon kosher salt
1 teaspoon black pepper
½ teaspoon dried thyme leaves

1 teaspoon kosher salt
1 teaspoon black pepper

Prepare the EGG to cook indirect with a drip pan at 375°F. Place the pork, skin side down, on a cutting board. With a sharp, pointy knife, poke 6 deep, evenly spaced X-shaped incisions in the thickest parts of the pork. With your finger, stretch the holes so the garlic paste can be pushed in.

To make the paste, combine all of the ingredients in a small bowl and mix well. Using your finger, push some of the garlic paste deeply into each hole, distributing it evenly among all of the holes. Season the exposed meat with the salt and pepper.

Place the pork, skin side down, on the EGG cooking grid and cook for about 3½ hours, or until the internal temperature reaches 190°F deep in the thickest part.

Transfer the pork to a platter, tent loosely with aluminum foil, and let rest for 20 to 30 minutes. Remove and discard the skin and trim away any excessive fat. Slice the picnic against the grain ½ inch thick to serve.

A roasted ham is a great way to feed a crowd and nearly everybody seems to like it. Ham is a good value and can be adapted to many great flavors. I've often cooked mine in the EGG glazed with barbecue sauce, and in this recipe, I take that method a step further and incorporate some of the great flavors of a margarita. It all works: the sweet, the sour, the tequila, and the saltiness of a ham. I really think that this is going to be a fan favorite recipe on Cinco de Mayo and beyond. Olé!

Roasted Ham Glazed with Cabo Barbecue Sauce

MAKES ABOUT 10 SERVINGS

Prepare the EGG to cook indirect with a drip pan at 325°F. Dry the ham very well. Place the ham, cut side down, on the EGG cooking grid and cook for 30 minutes.

Meanwhile, make the glaze. Combine all of the ingredients in a medium bowl and whisk until well blended. Pour half of the glaze into a small microwave-safe bowl. Cover and reserve for serving with the ham. Brush the remaining half of the glaze all over the ham. Continue cooking and glazing every 30 minutes for about 2 hours total, or until the ham reaches an internal temperature of 160°F deep in the center.

Transfer the ham to a platter and let rest for 10 minutes. Discard any glaze that remains from the glazing bowl. Heat the reserved glaze in the microwave just until hot. Slice the ham and serve with the hot glaze.

1 (6 to 7-pound) bone-in fully cooked ham

GLAZE

2 cups ketchup

½ cup Cabo Tequila Blanco

¼ cup agave nectar

Juice of 1 lime

2 tablespoons hot sauce

1 teaspoon granulated garlic

1 teaspoon granulated onion

This is just good old roast beef. It's a classic Sunday dinner and that makes for great roast beef sandwiches on Monday. Make sure to buy USDA choice or prime meat for this recipe or it will be tough. Be very attentive to the internal temperature of the roast and to the required resting time to ensure a good result. You'll need a sharp knife and a steady hand to slice the roast thinly, but the payoff is a great meal.

Sunday Roast Beef MAKES ABOUT 6 SERVINGS

1 (3½-pound) sirloin tip roast

1 large clove garlic, cut lengthwise into 6 slivers

2 tablespoons olive oil

RUB

1 teaspoon kosher salt

1 teaspoon black pepper

½ teaspoon granulated garlic

½ teaspoon granulated onion

½ teaspoon paprika

GRAVY

2 tablespoons salted butter

2 tablespoons all-purpose flour

1¾ cups beef broth

¼ cup red wine

½ teaspoon black pepper

Prepare the EGG to cook indirect with a drip pan at 375°F. With a sharp, pointy knife, stab the roast deeply in 6 evenly spaced spots. Push a sliver of garlic deep into each of the holes. Rub the oil all over the roast. To make the rub, combine all of the ingredients in a small bowl and mix well. Season the roast on all sides with the rub, using it all.

Place the roast in the EGG and cook for about 1 hour and 15 minutes, or until it reaches an internal temperature deep in the center of 125°F for medium-rare.

Meanwhile, make the gravy. Melt the butter in a medium saucepan over medium heat on the stove. Add the flour and cook, stirring often, until fully incorporated. Gradually add the broth and wine while stirring constantly. Season with the pepper and bring to a simmer. Cook, stirring occasionally, for about 5 minutes, or until thickened. Check for salt and add if necessary.

When the roast is ready, transfer it to a platter, tent loosely with aluminum foil, and let rest for 15 minutes. Slice thinly and serve with the gravy on the side.

Pot roast is definitely comfort food at its best. Everyone loves pot roast, and that little flavor kick from roasting it on the EGG makes this one better than mom's. The herbs and touch of barbecue sauce contribute to a unique pot roast taste. This recipe would be great if you substituted venison or elk for a game version. Please invite me if you do.

Pot Roast with Potatoes and Carrots

MAKES ABOUT 4 SERVINGS

Prepare the EGG to cook indirect with a drip pan at 350°F with pecan wood added for smoke flavor. Season the roast all over with salt and pepper. Place the roast in the EGG and cook for 45 minutes.

Meanwhile, in a medium bowl, combine the broth, cornstarch, barbecue sauce, soy sauce, black pepper, and marjoram and whisk until well blended. When the roast is ready, transfer it to a 9 by 13-inch EGG-safe pan (or one roughly that size). Place the carrots and potatoes evenly around the roast. Sprinkle the onion and garlic evenly over the top of the roast. Whisk the broth mixture again to make sure it is well blended and then pour it over the top. Cover the pan with aluminum foil, sealing it tightly, and place it on the EGG cooking grid. Cook for 2½ hours, and then check the meat, carrots, and potatoes for tenderness. If they aren't all tender yet, cook for another 30 minutes, or until they are.

Remove the pan from the EGG. Transfer the roast to a platter and then surround it with the carrots and potatoes. Transfer the gravy to a pitcher and skim any fat off the top if desired. Check the gravy for salt and add if needed, then serve the gravy alongside the roast and vegetables.

1 (3½-pound) boneless beef chuck roast

Kosher salt and black pepper

2 cups beef broth

2 tablespoons cornstarch

2 tablespoons barbecue sauce

1 tablespoon soy sauce

½ teaspoon black pepper

½ teaspoon dried marjoram leaves

4 medium carrots, peeled and cut crosswise into thirds

4 medium russet potatoes, peeled and halved crosswise

1 cup finely chopped red onion

2 cloves garlic, crushed

Julia was my grandma who inspired me to cook good things. She only did it to feed the family and would be truly amazed at how my life has played out. She was born in France and cooked like a Frenchman. In her kitchen, no drippings ever didn't become a sauce. She often used tomato sauce to fortify her sauces, probably because that was what was available. However, once you try this garlicky lamb-based gravy, you will agree that it works. Grandma never saw a Big Green Egg, but I'm proud to use her influence in my cooking on it every day.

MAKES 6 TO 8 SERVINGS Leg of Lamb à la Julia

Prepare the EGG to cook indirect at 375°F. With a sharp, pointy knife, stab the roast deeply in 6 evenly spaced spots in the thickest parts of the lamb. Cut 1 clove of the garlic lengthwise into 6 slivers and stuff a sliver deeply into each hole. Season the lamb liberally all over with salt and pepper. Crush the remaining 4 garlic cloves and transfer them to the center of an EGG-safe pan. Add the onions to the garlic, mix well, and mound in the center of the pan. Drizzle the oil over the onion mixture, then place the lamb on top of it.

Place the pan in the EGG and cook for 1½ hours, or until the lamb is golden brown.

In a medium bowl, combine the tomato sauce, wine, basil, the ½ teaspoon salt, and the ½ teaspoon pepper and mix well. Pour the tomato mixture over the lamb. Cover the pan with aluminum foil, sealing it tightly, and continue to cook for about 1 hour longer, or until the lamb reaches an internal temperature of 180°F. This is well done by most standards, but this is how Julia did it and how I like it.

Remove the pan from the EGG and let the lamb rest for 15 minutes. Transfer the lamb to a cutting board and slice thinly against the grain. Spoon the sauce over the lamb slices and the pasta.

1 (4-pound) center-cut bone-in leg of lamb

5 cloves garlic, divided

½ teaspoon kosher salt, plus more for seasoning meat

½ teaspoon black pepper, plus more for seasoning meat

2 small yellow onions, finely chopped

1 tablespoon olive oil

1 cup tomato sauce

¼ cup red wine

½ teaspoon dried basil leaves

Cooked pasta, for serving

This recipe looks simple but the result is juicy chicken with a nicely browned skin and that coveted crunch. Crispy skin is something everyone loves on chicken, and it's easy to achieve with an EGG. Hot roasting is a fun way to cook, so don't think that you have to cook only low and slow with the convEGGtor. You can safely fire up the EGG to 550°F and beyond. I am using thighs here and I often use legs. They can take the high heat better than white meat.

Hot-Roasted Crispy Chicken Thighs MAKES ABOUT 4 SERVINGS

8 chicken thighs

RUB

1½ teaspoons kosher salt

1 teaspoon black pepper

1 teaspoon paprika

1 teaspoon granulated onion

1 teaspoon granulated garlic

Prepare the EGG to cook indirect at 550°F. To make the rub, combine all of the ingredients in a small bowl and mix well. Season the chicken on all sides with the rub, using it all.

Place the chicken in the EGG and cook for 30 to 35 minutes, until it reaches an internal temperature of 195°F and the skin is crispy. Serve immediately while the skin is hot and crispy.

A turkey cooked on the EGG is a real treat. It's simple and the wood flavor from the charcoal makes it delicious. I don't like any added wood, but many folks do, so you may want to add a little bit of apple or cherry wood. I have been using Butterball turkeys for many years and never brine them, as they're always tender and juicy. I'm going to keep using them and recommend that you use them, too. The ice-bag trick I use here came to me from old EGGhead friend Max Rosen. The ice cools the white meat down ahead of time so it cooks a little slower and gets done at the same time as the dark meat.

Happy Thanksgiving Turkey

MAKES ABOUT 10 SERVINGS

Remove the giblets and neck from the turkey. Dry the bird well inside and out with paper towels. Tuck its wings behind its back in a triangle fashion. Place the turkey breast side up on a large platter. Fill a gallon-size heavy-duty resealable plastic bag three-fourths full with ice cubes. Lay the bag on top of the turkey breast and let rest at room temperature for 1 hour.

Prepare the EGG to cook indirect with a drip pan at 325°F. Remove the ice bag and discard the bag and the ice. Rub the turkey all over with oil. Season the turkey all over, inside and out, with salt and pepper. Place the onion and apple inside the cavity.

Place the turkey, breast side up, on the EGG cooking grid and cook until the turkey reaches an internal temperature of 160°F deep in the breast down by the wing joint and 180°F deep in the thigh. This will take about 4 hours, but it's critical to use the internal temperature as your guide to doneness.

Transfer the turkey to a platter, tent loosely with aluminum foil, and let rest for 20 minutes. Carve and serve.

1 (15-pound) turkey, fully defrosted
Ice cubes
Olive oil, for rubbing
Kosher salt and black pepper
1 small yellow onion, quartered
1 small Jonathan apple, quartered

Roasted duck somehow became a delicacy in the United States and that doesn't really make sense. It's tasty and easy to cook, but somehow it gets delegated to special occasions and Chinese restaurants. Well, enough of that. Everyone needs to start cooking it more often, and this EGG-roasted duck is a great place to start. If you like, spice up the glaze with a little more Sriracha sauce, and make an extra batch for dipping, too. This would be a fine place to add a bit of cherry wood to the roasting for a light smoke flavor.

EGG Roasted Duck MAKES 2 SERVINGS

1 (5-pound) duck
Kosher salt and black pepper
1 small yellow onion, quartered

GLAZE
½ cup orange marmalade
2 tablespoons soy sauce
1½ teaspoons Sriracha sauce

Prepare the EGG to cook indirect with a drip pan at 350°F. Dry the duck well and trim off any extra fat or skin. With a sharp, pointy knife, prick the skin of the duck all over at ½-inch intervals, trying not to cut into the meat at all. This will help drain the fat as it cooks. Season the duck liberally inside and out with salt and black pepper. Place the onion in the cavity and tie the legs together with kitchen string.

Place the duck, breast side up, on a rack in an EGG-safe pan. Place the pan on the EGG cooking grid and cook for 1 hour. Raise the temperature of the EGG to 400°F and continue cooking for 1 hour longer.

Meanwhile, make the glaze. Combine all of the ingredients in a small bowl and whisk until smooth. After the second hour of cooking, glaze the duck on all sides with a thick coating of the glaze. Raise the temperature of the EGG to 450°F and continue to cook for about another 30 to 40 minutes, until the skin is crispy and the duck is cooked to an internal temperature of 180°F deep in the breast.

Remove the pan from the EGG and let rest for 5 minutes. Carve to serve.

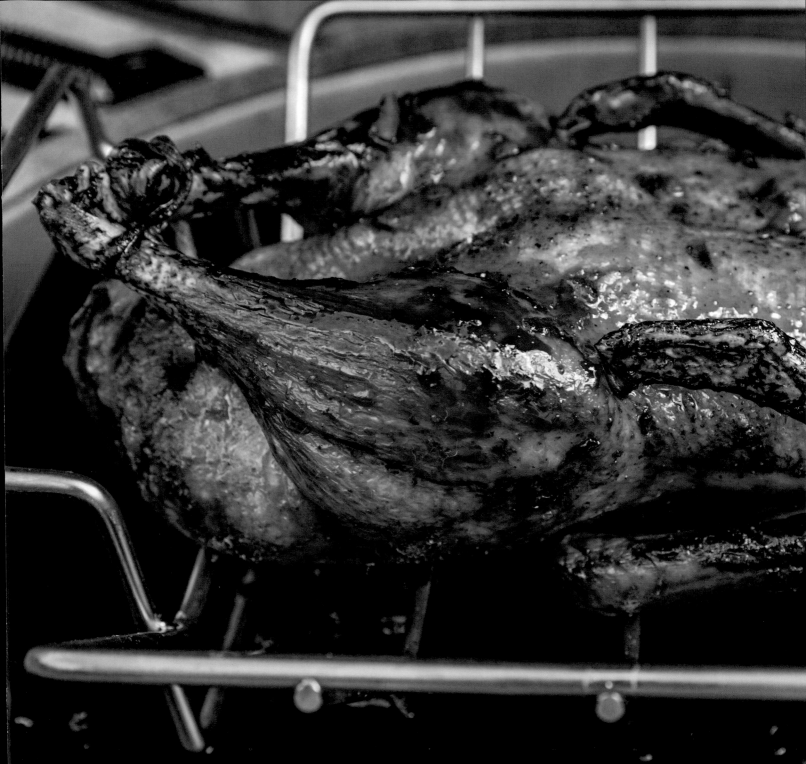

Little red creamer potatoes are smooth, tasty, and perfect for roasting. Mine are highly seasoned and they wear it well. Be sure to get fresh rosemary for that extra kick, and cook the potatoes until they are as brown as you like them. At my house that's usually a little browner than most. We love those crunchy edges and lots of caramelization. I'd serve these potatoes with anything from bacon and eggs to a holiday prime rib dinner and be very happy.

Little Red Potatoes MAKES ABOUT 4 SERVINGS

5 cups halved little red potatoes
  (about 2½ pounds)

¼ cup olive oil

RUB

2 teaspoons kosher salt

1 teaspoon black pepper

1 teaspoon granulated garlic

1 teaspoon granulated onion

1 teaspoon paprika

1 tablespoon chopped
  fresh rosemary

Prepare the EGG to cook indirect at 450°F. Put the potatoes in a large bowl. Drizzle the oil over the potatoes and toss to coat evenly. To make the rub, combine all of the ingredients in a small bowl and mix well. Sprinkle the rub over the potatoes and toss to coat evenly. Place the potatoes in an EGG-safe 9 by 13-inch pan (or one roughly that size).

Place the pan in the EGG and cook for 20 minutes. Toss the potatoes to ensure even cooking and cook for another 20 to 30 minutes, until soft and golden brown. Serve hot.

Roasting a whole head of cauliflower makes for a great presentation, but this is not your grandma's cauliflower. It's not boiled to death and it's not bathing in beloved cheese sauce. This is cooked and served whole, it's a little crunchy at the stalk, and it's glazed with barbecue sauce with a bit of an Asian flair to it. I'd say it's the polar opposite of your grandma's, but it's a real winner and I think you will make this often. If you just can't handle cooking it whole, go ahead and cut the florets off, but roast them the same way.

Roasted Head of Cauliflower

MAKES 4 SERVINGS

Prepare the EGG to cook indirect at 375°F. Trim the green leaves away and flatten the bottom of the stem so the cauliflower will sit upright. Place the cauliflower in a medium EGG-safe pan and brush it all over with the oil. To make the rub, combine all of the ingredients in a small bowl and mix well. Season the cauliflower liberally all over with the rub, using it all. Cover the pan tightly with aluminum foil. Pour the broth in the bottom of the pan. Place the pan in the EGG and cook for 1 hour.

Remove the pan from the EGG and remove the foil. To make the glaze, combine all of the ingredients in a medium bowl and whisk until well blended. Brush the cauliflower all over with the glaze. Do not re-cover the pan with foil. Return the pan to the EGG and cook for about 1 hour, or until the cauliflower is tender in the center when poked with a long skewer. Transfer to a bowl to serve.

1 large head cauliflower

2 tablespoons olive oil

RUB

1 teaspoon granulated onion

½ teaspoon granulated garlic

½ teaspoon kosher salt

½ teaspoon black pepper

½ cup vegetable broth

GLAZE

½ cup ketchup

2 teaspoons soy sauce

2 teaspoons toasted sesame oil

1 teaspoon Sriracha sauce

1 teaspoon honey

When we see winter squashes showing up at the supermarket, we know fall is here. As a cook, it's always good to look for seasonal food that's grown near where you live. Nowadays this is talked about as a culinary concept, but it's really just common sense. So when you see butternut squashes piling up, it's time to cook some of them. They're tasty and healthy and easy to cook. This is a simple roasting recipe with a little bit of barbecue sauce added for the glaze.

Roasted Butternut Squash
MAKES 6 SERVINGS

Prepare the EGG to cook indirect at 400°F. Using a vegetable peeler, peel the squash. Using a sharp knife, cut off the stem and then cut the squash in half lengthwise. Using a spoon, scoop out and discard the seeds. Cut the squash into bite-size chunks and put them in a bowl. Drizzle the oil over the squash and toss to coat evenly. Sprinkle the salt, pepper, and barbecue rub over the squash and toss to coat evenly. Drizzle the barbecue sauce over the squash and again toss to coat evenly. Spray a round perforated grid with vegetable cooking spray. Spread the squash evenly on the prepared grid.

Place the grid in the EGG and cook for 20 minutes. Toss the squash to ensure even cooking and cook for another 20 to 30 minutes, until soft to the touch and golden brown.

Transfer the squash to a bowl and drizzle with the butter. Toss to coat evenly and serve.

1 medium butternut squash

2 tablespoons olive oil

1 teaspoon kosher salt

1 teaspoon black pepper

1 teaspoon barbecue rub

¼ cup sweet barbecue sauce

4 tablespoons salted butter, melted

I admit that I don't cook or eat a lot of green stuff, but as a cookbook author, it's important to include things that aren't my personal favorite because you may actually like them. I tried my best to cook these in a way that a vegetarian would like them, but I couldn't resist adding some bacon and cheese at the end. I even tasted the sprouts when they were done, and I have to admit that they were pretty good. It must have been the addition of the bacon.

Roasted Brussels Sprouts with Bacon MAKES 4 TO 6 SERVINGS

1 pound brussels sprouts

2 tablespoons olive oil

½ teaspoon kosher salt

½ teaspoon black pepper

½ teaspoon granulated garlic

Juice of ¼ lemon

2 slices bacon, cooked and crumbled

¼ cup grated Parmesan cheese

Prepare the EGG to cook indirect at 400°F. Check the sprouts and trim off any brown stems and discard any yellow leaves. Place the sprouts in a bowl, drizzle with the oil, and toss to coat evenly. In a small bowl, combine the salt, pepper, and granulated garlic and mix well. Sprinkle the salt mixture over the sprouts and toss to coat evenly. Spray a large round perforated grid with vegetable cooking spray. Spread the sprouts on the prepared grid, spacing them evenly.

Place the grid in the EGG and cook for 20 minutes. Toss the sprouts to ensure even cooking and cook for another 20 minutes, or until soft and golden brown.

Transfer the sprouts to a bowl and drizzle with the lemon juice. Top with the bacon and Parmesan and toss to coat evenly. To serve, transfer the sprouts to a shallow bowl and top with any bacon or cheese left behind in the bowl.

The Christmas classic roasted chestnuts take on a whole new dimension when you cook them in the EGG. The kids will love joining in to remove the woody shells. Peel them quickly while they are still warm or it will be tough to get the shell off, though a little reheat will soften them right back up. I like orange marmalade as an accompaniment, but any sweet dip will work. Be sure to serve hot chocolate and sing Christmas carols to complete the scene.

Christmas Chestnuts MAKES ABOUT 4 SERVINGS

1 pound chestnuts

Orange marmalade, for dipping

Prepare the EGG to cook indirect at 425°F. Using a sharp serrated knife, cut a ½-inch-long X in the rounded side of each chestnut. Place the chestnuts, cut side up, on a round perforated grid.

Place the grid in the EGG and roast the chestnuts for 15 to 20 minutes, until the shells burst open and curl away from the nut meats. Transfer the hot chestnuts to a kitchen towel, wrap them in the towel, and squeeze gently to loosen the shells further. Let rest, wrapped, for 5 minutes.

Peel the chestnuts and serve immediately or let the guests peel them themselves. Serve with marmalade for dipping.

My mom made a couple of hundred of these in my life and always cooked them in the oven with just a little salt and pepper. Mine gets a tasty rub and that great flavor from the EGG. She also overcooked them, just like everybody's mom did to ward off the evil things that lurked within. Nowadays, of course, we know that pork is perfectly fine cooked a little pink. I cook lean pork to 150°F, but because this roast is kind of fatty, I cook it a little more. Just give it a five-minute rest after cooking and it will be perfect.

MAKES ABOUT 6 SERVINGS Classic Pork Roast

One hour before you plan to cook, take the roast out of the refrigerator. Prepare the EGG to cook indirect with a drip pan at 350°F.

To make the rub, combine all of the ingredients in a small bowl and mix well. Season the roast on all sides with the rub, using it all. Let the roast rest at room temperature for 15 to 30 minutes.

In a small bowl, combine the onion, garlic, and oil and mix well. Pile this onion mixture in the middle of an EGG-safe pan. Place the roast on top of the onion mixture and place the pan in the EGG. Cook for about 2 hours, or until the roast reaches an internal temperature of 155°F deep in the center.

Transfer the roast to a platter, tent loosely with aluminum foil, and let rest for 5 to 10 minutes. Slice thickly with the bones intact for a prime rib type of meal, or separate the bones and slice thinly to serve family-style. Drizzle the onions and accumulated juices over the meat before serving.

1 (4-pound) bone-in pork loin rib end roast

RUB
1 teaspoon kosher salt
½ teaspoon black pepper
½ teaspoon paprika
½ teaspoon granulated garlic
¼ teaspoon granulated onion
¼ teaspoon raw sugar
¼ teaspoon dried thyme leaves

1 medium yellow onion, finely chopped
2 cloves garlic, crushed
1 tablespoon olive oil

METRIC CONVERSIONS AND EQUIVALENTS

Metric Conversion Formulas

To Convert	Multiply
Ounces to grams	Ounces by 28.35
Pounds to kilograms	Pounds by .454
Teaspoons to milliliters	Teaspoons by 4.93
Tablespoons to milliliters	Tablespoons by 14.79
Fluid ounces to milliliters	Fluid ounces by 29.57
Cups to milliliters	Cups by 236.59
Cups to liters	Cups by .236
Pints to liters	Pints by .473
Quarts to liters	Quarts by .946
Gallons to liters	Gallons by 3.785
Inches to centimeters	Inches by 2.54

Common Ingredients and Their Approximate Equivalents

1 cup uncooked white rice = 185 grams

1 cup all-purpose flour = 125 grams

1 stick butter (4 ounces • ½ cup • 8 tablespoons) = 115 grams

1 cup butter (8 ounces • 2 sticks • 16 tablespoons) = 225 grams

1 cup brown sugar (firmly packed) = 220 grams

1 cup granulated sugar = 200 grams

Oven Temperatures

To convert Fahrenheit to Celsius, subtract 32 from Fahrenheit, multiply the result by 5, then divide by 9.

Description	Fahrenheit	Celsius	British Gas Mark
Very cool	200°	95°	0
Very cool	225°	110°	¼
Very cool	250°	120°	½
Cool	275°	135°	1
Cool	300°	150°	2
Warm	325°	165°	3
Moderate	350°	175°	4
Moderately hot	375°	190°	5
Fairly hot	400°	200°	6
Hot	425°	220°	7
Very hot	450°	230°	8
Very hot	475°	245°	9

Approximate Metric Equivalents

Volume

¼ teaspoon	1 milliliter
½ teaspoon	2.5 milliliters
¾ teaspoon	4 milliliters
1 teaspoon	5 milliliters
1¼ teaspoons	6 milliliters
1½ teaspoons	7.5 milliliters
1¾ teaspoons	8.5 milliliters
2 teaspoons	10 milliliters
1 tablespoon (½ fluid ounce)	15 milliliters
2 tablespoons (1 fluid ounce)	30 milliliters
¼ cup	60 milliliters
⅓ cup	80 milliliters
½ cup (4 fluid ounces)	120 milliliters
⅔ cup	160 milliliters
¾ cup	180 milliliters
1 cup (8 fluid ounces)	240 milliliters
1¼ cups	300 milliliters
1½ cups (12 fluid ounces)	360 milliliters
1⅔ cups	400 milliliters
2 cups (1 pint)	460 milliliters
3 cups	700 milliliters
4 cups (1 quart)	0.95 liter
1 quart plus ¼ cup	1 liter
4 quarts (1 gallon)	3.8 liters

Weight

¼ ounce	7 grams
½ ounce	14 grams
¾ ounce	21 grams
1 ounce	28 grams
1¼ ounces	35 grams
1½ ounces	42.5 grams
1⅔ ounces	45 grams
2 ounces	57 grams
3 ounces	85 grams
4 ounces (¼ pound)	113 grams
5 ounces	142 grams
6 ounces	170 grams
7 ounces	198 grams
8 ounces (½ pound)	227 grams
16 ounces (1 pound)	454 grams
35.25 ounces (2.2 pounds)	1 kilogram

Length

⅛ inch	3 millimeters
¼ inch	6 millimeters
½ inch	12 millimeters
1 inch	2.5 centimeters
2 inches	5 centimeters
2½ inches	6 centimeters
4 inches	10 centimeters
5 inches	13 centimeters
6 inches	15 centimeters
12 inches (1 foot)	30 centimeters

Information compiled from a variety of sources, including *Recipes into Type* by Joan Whitman and Dolores Simon (Newton, MA: Biscuit Books, 1993); *The New Food Lover's Companion* by Sharon Tyler Herbst (Hauppauge, NY: Barron's, 2013); and *Rosemary Brown's Big Kitchen Instruction Book* (Kansas City, MO: Andrews McMeel, 1998).

INDEX

A

almonds, 58
aluminum foil pans, 13
appetizers. *See also* salads; snacks;
    soup
    Chorizo and Shrimpo Fundido, 56
    Florida-Style Smoked Fish Spread,
    52
    Gyro Meatballs with Tzatziki, 119
    Ham and Cheese Toasty, 104
    Ham and Swiss Cheese Poppers, 55
    Pepper Jelly Meat Loaf Cupcakes, 98
    Smoked Jalapeño Hummus, 54
    Smoke-Kissed Deviled Eggs, 53
apple wood, 7
apples, 113
ash management, 7
asparagus, 49

B

Baby Back Ribs with Cookie Butter
    Barbecue Sauce, 68–69
bacon
    Bacon and Egg Cheeseburgers,
    28, 29
    Roasted Brussels Sprouts with
    Bacon, 136, 137
Baked Lobster Tails, 105
baking, 81
    Baked Lobster Tails, 105
    Blueberry French Toast Casserole,
    82, 83
    Caramel Baked Apples, 113
    Deep-Dish Tourist Pizza, 88–89
    Fully Loaded Calzone, 94–95

Ginny and Kim's Deep-Dish Pizza
    Dough, 86
Ginny and Kim's Dessert Pizza,
    92–93
Ginny and Kim's Pizza Sauce, 87
Ginny and Kim's Thin-Crust Pizza
    Dough, 85
Green Velvet Cake, 110
Ham and Cheese Toasty, 104
Homemade Garlic Knots, 96, 97
Mac and Cheeseburger Casserole,
    100
Pepper Jelly Meat Loaf Cupcakes, 98
pizza, 84
Scalloped Potatoes with Ham, 101
Southern Chicken Bog, 99
Stuffmuffins, 107
Summertime Zucchini Pie, 102, 103
Swiss Cheesy Double-Baked
    Potatoes, 106
Tennessee Honey-Caramel Pecan
    Pie, 111
Thin-Crust Real Chicago Pizza,
    90, 91
White Chocolate Chip–Cherry
    Cookies, 108, 109
Wrapped S'mores, 112
barbecue
    Barbecue Beef Sammiches, 60, 61
    Barbecued Pork Shoulder with
    Carolina Sauce, 78–79
barbecue competition, 2
barbecue sauce
    Cabo Barbecue Sauce, 123
    Cookie Butter Barbecue Sauce,
    68–69

BBQ Forum, 1
beans
    Chunky Chili Con Carne, 62–63
    Smoked Jalapeño Hummus, 54
    Smoked White Beans with Turkey
    and Kale, 59
beef
    Barbecue Beef Sammiches, 60, 61
    Beef Tips in Double Onion Gravy, 75
    Better Than Any Steak House Rib
    Eye, 33
    Chunky Chili Con Carne, 62–63
    doneness, 11
    Dr. BBQ's Smoked Meatball Gumbo,
    65–66
    Filet Mignon with Blue Cheese
    Butter, 34, 35
    Flat-Iron Steak Salad, 20–21
    Grilled Tri-Tip with Chunky Steak
    Sauce, 36
    Herbed-Up Prime Rib, 120, 121
    Mac and Cheeseburger Casserole,
    100
    Pepper Jelly Meat Loaf Cupcakes, 98
    Pot Roast with Potatoes and Carrots,
    125
    Sunday Roast Beef, 124
    Texas-Style Beef Brisket, 73
Better Than Any Steak House Rib Eye,
    33
Big Green Egg DigiQ, 13
Big Green Egg Forum, 1
blender, 13
Blue Cheese Butter, 34, 35
Blueberry French Toast Casserole, 82, 83

Boom Boom Shrimp Wraps, 27
bottom vent, 8
bread. *See also* pizza
  Homemade Garlic Knots, 96, 97
breakfast, 82, 83
brine, 46, 77
  Brined and Smoked Turkey Thighs,
    67
brisket
  doneness, 11
  Red Chile Brisket, 74
  Texas-Style Beef Brisket, 73
Brown Sugar Vinaigrette, 20–21
brussels sprouts, 136, 137
burgers
  Bacon and Egg Cheeseburgers,
    28, 29
  Mac and Cheeseburger Casserole,
    100
  Triple Pork Burgers, 31
Burson, Jodi, ix, 3
butter
  Blue Cheese Butter, 34, 35
  Cookie Butter Barbecue Sauce,
    68–69
  Fun Butter, 48
butternut squash, 134, 135

C

Cabo Barbecue Sauce, 123
Cabo-rita Chicken Tacos, 44, 45
cake, 110
calzone, 94–95
Caramel Baked Apples, 113
Carolina Sauce, 78–79
carrots, 125
casserole
  Blueberry French Toast Casserole,
    82, 83

Mac and Cheeseburger Casserole,
  100
cast-iron Dutch oven, 13
cauliflower, 133
charcoal, 6, 13
Charred Ranchero Sauce, 40–41
cheese
  Blue Cheese Butter, 34, 35
  Chorizo and Shrimpo Fundido, 56, 57
  Ham and Cheese Toasty, 104
  Ham and Swiss Cheese Poppers, 55
  Parmesan Grits, 42
  Swiss Cheesy Double-Baked
    Potatoes, 106
cheeseburgers
  Bacon and Egg Cheeseburgers, 28,
    29
  Mac and Cheeseburger Casserole,
    100
cherries, 108, 109
cherry wood, 7
chestnuts, 138
chicken
  Cabo-rita Chicken Tacos, 44, 45
  Chicken Wings with Pink Sauce, 18
  doneness, 11
  Fiery Jerk Chicken Legs, 43
  Hot-Roasted Crispy Chicken Thighs,
    128
  Southern Chicken Bog, 99
chile, 74
chili, 62–63
chili powder, 14
Chopped Grill Masters, 40
Chorizo and Shrimpo Fundido, 56, 57
Christmas Chestnuts, 138
Chunky Chili Con Carne, 62–63
Chunky Steak Sauce, 36

cilantro, 37
Classic Pork Roast, 139
convEGGtor, 5
Cookie Butter Barbecue Sauce, 68–69
cookies, 108, 109
cooking setups, 10
cooking temperature, 8–9, 11
corn, 48
Cornish hens, 46–47
Crispy Lobster Quesadilla, 25
cupcakes, 98
cutting board, 13

D

D'Amico, Rob (Guido), 84
deep-dish pizza dough, 86
Deep-Dish Tourist Pizza, 88–89
dessert
  Caramel Baked Apples, 113
  Ginny and Kim's Dessert Pizza,
    92–93
  Green Velvet Cake, 110
  White Chocolate Chip–Cherry
    Cookies, 108, 109
  Wrapped S'mores, 112
deviled eggs, 53
DigiQ, 13
direct cooking, 5, 10, 17
doneness, 11
Double Onion Gravy, 75
Dr. BBQ's Smoked Meatball Gumbo,
  65–66
dressing, 20–21
dried cherries, 108, 109
drip pan, 10
dry rubs. *See* rubs
duck, 130, 131

E

The Egg and I, 1
EGG Roasted Duck, 130, 131
EGG Roasted Garlic Soup, 116–17
EGG sizes, 5
EGG Smoked Salmon, 76, 77
EGGcessories, 5, 9
EGGfests, 84, 110
EGGheads, ix, 1–4, 17, 55, 84, 110, 115, 129
eggs
    Bacon and Egg Cheeseburgers, 28, 29
    Smoke-Kissed Deviled Eggs, 53
EGGzpacho, 19

F

Fiery Jerk Chicken Legs, 43
Fiery Swordfish Tacos, 26
Filet Mignon with Blue Cheese Butter, 34, 35
fish. *See* seafood
Fisher, Ed, 3, 5
flashback, 10
Flat-Iron Steak Salad, 20–21
Florida BBQ Association, 1
Florida-Style Smoked Fish Spread, 52
Food Fighters, 40
food processor, 13
French toast casserole, 82, 83
fruit
    Blueberry French Toast Casserole, 82, 83
    Caramel Baked Apples, 113
    dried cherries, 108, 109
    Grilled Peach and Serrano Salsa, 24
    Grilled Watermelon Salad, 22–23
    Savory Grilled Pears, 38, 39
Fully Loaded Calzone, 94–95
Fun Butter, 48

G

garlic soup, 116–17
gazpacho. *See* Eggzpacho
Ginny and Kim's Deep-Dish Pizza Dough, 86
Ginny and Kim's Dessert Pizza, 92–93
Ginny and Kim's Pizza Sauce, 87
Ginny and Kim's Thin-Crust Pizza Dough, 85
glaze, 14, 123, 130, 133
    Maple Whiskey Glaze, 32
gloves, 13
gravy, 65–66, 124
    Double Onion Gravy, 75
Green Velvet Cake, 110
Grilled Peach and Serrano Salsa, 24
Grilled Veal Chops with Parmesan Grits, 42
grilling, 10, 17
    Bacon and Egg Cheeseburgers, 28, 29
    Better Than Any Steak House Rib Eye, 33
    Boom Boom Shrimp Wraps, 27
    Cabo-rita Chicken Tacos, 44, 45
    Chicken Wings with Pink Sauce, 18
    Crispy Lobster Quesadilla, 25
    EGGzpacho, 19
    Fiery Jerk Chicken Legs, 43
    Fiery Swordfish Tacos, 26
    Filet Mignon with Blue Cheese Butter, 34, 35
    Flat-Iron Steak Salad, 20–21
    Grilled Peach and Serrano Salsa, 24
    Grilled Sweet Corn with Fun Butter, 48
    Grilled Tri-Tip with Chunky Steak Sauce, 36
    Grilled Veal Chops with Parmesan Grits, 42
    Grilled Watermelon Salad, 22–23
    Lamb Chops with Mint-Cilantro Pesto, 37
    Pork Tenderloin with Maple Whiskey Glaze, 32
    Porterhouse Pork Chops with Savory Grilled Pears, 38, 39
    Rib Eye Pork Chops with Charred Ranchero Sauce, 40–41
    Sandi's Fave Grilled Asparagus, 49
    Sliders with Homemade Italian Sausage, 30
    Spatchcocked and Grilled Cornish Hens, 46–47
    Triple Pork Burgers, 31
grits, 42
gumbo, 65–66
Gyro Meatballs with Tzatziki, 119

H

Hale, Marsha Manley, 111
ham
    Ham and Cheese Toasty, 104
    Ham and Swiss Cheese Poppers, 55
    Roasted Ham Glazed with Cabo Barbecue Sauce, 123
    Scalloped Potatoes with Ham, 101
Happy Thanksgiving Turkey, 129
Herbed-Up Prime Rib, 120, 121
hickory wood, 7
Homemade Garlic Knots, 96, 97
Homemade Italian Sausage, 30
Hot-Roasted Crispy Chicken Thighs, 128
hummus, 54

I

indirect cooking, 5, 10, 51, 81, 115
ingredients, 14
Italian sausage, 30

J

jalapeños, 54
jelly, pepper, 98
Jerk Paste, 43

K

kale, 59
Kansas City Steak Rub, 35
kitchen scale, 13
knives, 13

L

lamb
  doneness, 11
  Lamb Chops with Mint-Cilantro
    Pesto, 37
  Leg of Lamb à la Julia, 126, 127
Leg of Lamb à la Julia, 126, 127
lids, open or closed, 9
lighting, 8
Little Red Potatoes, 132
lobster
  Baked Lobster Tails, 105
  Crispy Lobster Quesadilla, 25
local meats, 14
lump charcoal, 6, 13

M

Mac and Cheeseburger Casserole, 100
MacDonald, Betty, 1
main dishes
  Baby Back Ribs with Cookie Butter
    Barbecue Sauce, 68–69
  Bacon and Egg Cheeseburgers, 28, 29

Baked Lobster Tails, 105
Barbecue Beef Sammiches, 60, 61
Barbecued Pork Shoulder with
  Carolina Sauce, 78–79
Beef Tips in Double Onion Gravy, 75
Better Than Any Steak House Rib
  Eye, 33
Boom Boom Shrimp Wraps, 27
Brined and Smoked Turkey Thighs, 67
Cabo-rita Chicken Tacos, 44, 45
Chicken Wings with Pink Sauce, 18
Chunky Chili Con Carne, 62–63
Classic Pork Roast, 139
Crispy Lobster Quesadilla, 25
Deep-Dish Tourist Pizza, 88–89
Dr. BBQ's Smoked Meatball Gumbo,
  65–66
EGG Roasted Duck, 130, 131
EGG Smoked Salmon, 76, 77
Fiery Jerk Chicken Legs, 43
Fiery Swordfish Tacos, 26
Filet Mignon with Blue Cheese But-
  ter, 34, 35
Fully Loaded Calzone, 94–95
Grilled Tri-Tip with Chunky Steak
  Sauce, 36
Grilled Veal Chops with Parmesan
  Grits, 42
Happy Thanksgiving Turkey, 129
Herbed-Up Prime Rib, 120, 121
Hot-Roasted Crispy Chicken Thighs,
  128
Lamb Chops with Mint-Cilantro
  Pesto, 37
Leg of Lamb à la Julia, 126, 127
Mac and Cheeseburger Casserole,
  100
Memphis Dry-Rubbed St. Louis–
  Style Ribs, 70, 71

Porchetta-Style Pork Roast, 118
Pork Tenderloin with Maple Whiskey
  Glaze, 32
Porterhouse Pork Chops with Savory
  Grilled Pears, 38, 39
Pot Roast with Potatoes and Carrots,
  125
Red Chile Brisket, 74
Rib Eye Pork Chops with Charred
  Ranchero Sauce, 40–41
Roasted Ham Glazed with Cabo
  Barbecue Sauce, 123
Roasted Pork Picnic, 122
Sliders with Homemade Italian
  Sausage, 30
Smoked White Beans with Turkey
  and Kale, 59
Southern Chicken Bog, 99
Spatchcocked and Grilled Cornish
  Hens, 46–47
Summertime Zucchini Pie, 102, 103
Sunday Roast Beef, 124
Tender and Tasty Pork Steaks, 72
Texas-Style Beef Brisket, 73
Thin-Crust Real Chicago Pizza, 90, 91
Triple Pork Burgers, 31
Maple Whiskey Glaze, 32
meat loaf cupcakes, 98
meatballs
  Dr. BBQ's Smoked Meatball Gumbo,
    65–66
  Gyro Meatballs with Tzatziki, 119
meats, 14. *See also specific type*
Memphis Dry-Rubbed St. Louis–Style
  Ribs, 70, 71
Mint-Cilantro Pesto, 37
mitts, 13
muffins, 107

N

Nicholas, Nick, 1
nitrile gloves, 13
nuts
Christmas Chestnuts, 138
Smokin' Almonds, 58
Tennessee Honey-Caramel
Pecan Pie, 111

O

oak wood, 7
onion gravy, 75

P

pans, 10, 13
Parmesan Grits, 42
pasta
Leg of Lamb à la Julia, 126, 127
Mac and Cheeseburger Casserole,
100
peaches, 24
pears, 38, 39
pecan pie, 111
pecan wood, 7
Pepper Jelly Meat Loaf Cupcakes, 98
perforated grids, 13
pesto, 37
pie
Summertime Zucchini Pie, 102, 103
Tennessee Honey-Caramel Pecan
Pie, 111
Pink Sauce, 18
pizza, 84. *See also* calzone
Deep-Dish Tourist Pizza, 88–89
Ginny and Kim's Deep-Dish Pizza
Dough, 86
Ginny and Kim's Dessert Pizza,
92–93
Ginny and Kim's Pizza Sauce, 87

Ginny and Kim's Thin-Crust Pizza
Dough, 85
pizza stone, 13
Thin-Crust Real Chicago Pizza, 90, 91
poppers, 55
Porchetta-Style Pork Roast, 118
pork, 14
Baby Back Ribs with Cookie Butter
Barbecue Sauce, 68–69
Barbecued Pork Shoulder with
Carolina Sauce, 78–79
Classic Pork Roast, 139
doneness, 11
Dr. BBQ's Smoked Meatball Gumbo,
65–66
Ham and Cheese Toasty, 104
Ham and Swiss Cheese Poppers, 55
Memphis Dry-Rubbed St. Louis–
Style Ribs, 70, 71
Porchetta-Style Pork Roast, 118
Pork Tenderloin with Maple Whiskey
Glaze, 32
Porterhouse Pork Chops with Savory
Grilled Pears, 38, 39
Rib Eye Pork Chops with Charred
Ranchero Sauce, 40–41
Roasted Ham Glazed with Cabo
Barbecue Sauce, 123
Roasted Pork Picnic, 122
Scalloped Potatoes with Ham, 101
Sliders with Homemade Italian
Sausage, 30
Stuffmuffins, 107
Tender and Tasty Pork Steaks, 72
Triple Pork Burgers, 31
Porterhouse Pork Chops with Savory
Grilled Pears, 38, 39
Pot Roast with Potatoes and Carrots,
125

potatoes
Little Red Potatoes, 132
Pot Roast with Potatoes and Carrots,
125
Scalloped Potatoes with Ham, 101
Swiss Cheesy Double-Baked
Potatoes, 106
prime rib, 120, 121
Pro Barbecue Grand Championship, 2
produce, 14
pulled beef, 60, 61

Q

quesadilla, 25

R

ranchero sauce, 40–41
Red Chile Brisket, 74
Rib Eye Pork Chops with Charred
Ranchero Sauce, 40–41
rib eye steak, 33
rib roast, 120, 121
ribs
Baby Back Ribs with Cookie Butter
Barbecue Sauce, 68–69
Memphis Dry-Rubbed St. Louis–
Style Ribs, 70, 71
Roasted Head of Cauliflower, 133
roasting, 115
Christmas Chestnuts, 138
Classic Pork Roast, 139
EGG Roasted Duck, 130, 131
EGG Roasted Garlic Soup, 116–17
Gyro Meatballs with Tzatziki, 119
Happy Thanksgiving Turkey, 129
Herbed-Up Prime Rib, 120, 121
Hot-Roasted Crispy Chicken Thighs,
128
Leg of Lamb à la Julia, 126, 127

Little Red Potatoes, 132
Porchetta-Style Pork Roast, 118
Pot Roast with Potatoes and Carrots, 125
Roasted Brussels Sprouts with Bacon, 136, 137
Roasted Butternut Squash, 134, 135
Roasted Ham Glazed with Cabo Barbecue Sauce, 123
Roasted Head of Cauliflower, 133
Roasted Pork Picnic, 122
Sunday Roast Beef, 124
Rosen, Max, 129
rubs
    for grilled dishes, 18, 20–21, 26, 31, 32, 33, 36, 38, 40–41, 44
    Jerk Paste, 43
    Kansas City Steak Rub, 35
    for roasted dishes, 124, 128, 132, 133, 139
    for smoked dishes, 60, 68–69, 70, 72, 78–79

S

salads
    Flat-Iron Steak Salad, 20–21
    Grilled Watermelon Salad, 22, 23
salmon, 76, 77
salsa, 26
    Grilled Peach and Serrano Salsa, 24
salt, 14
Sandi (fiancée), 49, 116
Sandi's Fave Grilled Asparagus, 49
sandwiches, 60, 61
sauce, 14, 26, 27, 29, 44, 60, 72. See also glaze; gravy
    Cabo Barbecue Sauce, 123
    Carolina Sauce, 78–79
    Charred Ranchero Sauce, 40–41

Chunky Steak Sauce, 36
Cookie Butter Barbecue Sauce, 68–69
Ginny and Kim's Pizza Sauce, 87
Grilled Peach and Serrano Salsa, 24
Mint-Cilantro Pesto, 37
Pink Sauce, 18
Red Chile Sauce, 74
tzatziki, 119
sausage
    Sliders with Homemade Italian Sausage, 30
    Stuffmuffins, 107
Savory Grilled Pears, 38, 39
scale, 13
Scalloped Potatoes with Ham, 101
seafood, 14
    Baked Lobster Tails, 105
    Boom Boom Shrimp Wraps, 27
    Chorizo and Shrimpo Fundido, 56, 57
    Crispy Lobster Quesadilla, 25
    EGG Smoked Salmon, 76, 77
    Fiery Swordfish Tacos, 26
    Florida-Style Smoked Fish Spread, 52
seasoning, 14
shrimp
    Boom Boom Shrimp Wraps, 27
    Chorizo and Shrimpo Fundido, 56, 57
side dishes
    Grilled Sweet Corn with Fun Butter, 48
    Homemade Garlic Knots, 96, 97
    Little Red Potatoes, 132
    Parmesan Grits, 42
    Roasted Brussels Sprouts with Bacon, 136, 137
    Roasted Butternut Squash, 134, 135

Roasted Head of Cauliflower, 133
Sandi's Fave Grilled Asparagus, 49
Savory Grilled Pears, 38, 39
Scalloped Potatoes with Ham, 101
Stuffmuffins, 107
Swiss Cheesy Double-Baked Potatoes, 106
silicone mitts, 13
Sliders with Homemade Italian Sausage, 30
smoking, 51
    Baby Back Ribs with Cookie Butter Barbecue Sauce, 68–69
    Barbecue Beef Sammiches, 60, 61
    Barbecued Pork Shoulder with Carolina Sauce, 78–79
    Beef Tips in Double Onion Gravy, 75
    Brined and Smoked Turkey Thighs, 67
    Chorizo and Shrimpo Fundido, 56, 57
    Chunky Chili Con Carne, 62, 63
    Dr. BBQ's Smoked Meatball Gumbo, 65–66
    EGG Smoked Salmon, 76, 77
    Florida-Style Smoked Fish Spread, 52
    Ham and Swiss Cheese Poppers, 55
    Memphis Dry-Rubbed St. Louis–Style Ribs, 70, 71
    Red Chile Brisket, 74
    Smoked Jalapeño Hummus, 54
    Smoked White Beans with Turkey and Kale, 59
    Smoke-Kissed Deviled Eggs, 53
    Smokin' Almonds, 58
    Tender and Tasty Pork Steaks, 72
    Texas-Style Beef Brisket, 73
s'mores, 112

snacks. *See also* appetizers
    Christmas Chestnuts, 138
    Ham and Cheese Toasty, 104
    Smokin' Almonds, 58
soup
    EGG Roasted Garlic Soup, 116–17
    EGGzpacho, 19
Southern Chicken Bog, 99
Spatchcocked and Grilled Cornish
    Hens, 46–47
speculoos spread, 68–69
spreads
    Florida-Style Smoked Fish Spread,
    52
    speculoos spread, 68–69
squash
    Roasted Butternut Squash, 134, 135
    Summertime Zucchini Pie, 102, 103
St. Louis–style ribs, 70, 71
steak
    Better Than Any Steak House Rib
    Eye, 33
    Filet Mignon with Blue Cheese
    Butter, 34, 35
    Flat-Iron Steak Salad, 20–21
    Grilled Tri-Tip with Chunky Steak
    Sauce, 36
    Tender and Tasty Pork Steaks, 72
Stuffmuffins, 107
Summertime Zucchini Pie, 102, 103
Sunday Roast Beef, 124
swiss cheese
    Ham and Swiss Cheese Poppers, 55
    Swiss Cheesy Double-Baked
    Potatoes, 106
swordfish, 26

T
tacos
    Cabo-rita Chicken Tacos, 44, 45
    Fiery Swordfish Tacos, 26
temperature, cooking, 8–9, 11
Tender and Tasty Pork Steaks, 72
Tennessee Honey-Caramel Pecan Pie,
    111
Texas-Style Beef Brisket, 73
thermometer, 13
thin-crust pizza dough
    Ginny and Kim's Thin-Crust Pizza
    Dough, 85
    Thin-Crust Real Chicago Pizza,
    90, 91
Tompkins, Brian, 2
tongs, 13
tools, 13
top vent, 8
Torres, Sue, 40
Triple Pork Burgers, 31
tri-tip, 36
turkey
    Brined and Smoked Turkey Thighs,
    67
    doneness, 11
    Happy Thanksgiving Turkey, 129
    Smoked White Beans with Turkey
    and Kale, 59
tzatziki, 119

V
veal chops, 42
vegetables. *See also* salads
    Grilled Sweet Corn with Fun Butter,
    48
    Little Red Potatoes, 132

    potatoes and carrots, 125
    Roasted Brussels Sprouts with
    Bacon, 136, 137
    Roasted Butternut Squash, 134, 135
    Roasted Head of Cauliflower, 133
    Sandi's Fave Grilled Asparagus, 49
    Scalloped Potatoes with Ham, 101
    Summertime Zucchini Pie, 102, 103
    Swiss Cheesy Double-Baked
    Potatoes, 106
venting, 7, 8
vinaigrette, 20–21
Vitamix blender, 13

W
watermelon salad, 22–23
West, Lou, 3
Whippen, Lee Anne, 38
whiskey glaze, 32
white beans, 59
White Chocolate Chip–Cherry
    Cookies, 108, 109
wings, 18
wood, 7, 13
World Barbecue Championship, 2
wraps
    Boom Boom Shrimp Wraps, 27
    Wrapped S'mores, 112

Y
Youngblood, Ginny, 84, 86, 92
Youngblood, Kim, 84, 86, 92

Z
zucchini pie, 102, 103